CURIOUS LONDON

Robin Cross is an author and journalist whose many books include the bestselling *VE-Day: Victory in Europe* and *We'll Meet Again* with Vera Lynn. He has also written a biography of President Kennedy, *JFK: A Hidden Life*. He is a regular contributor to the *Telegraph* and *Express* newspapers.

CURIOUS
London

A Guide to some
of the more unusual
delights of the capital

Robin Cross

PAN BOOKS

First published 1996 by Pan Books
an imprint of Macmillan General Books
25 Eccleston Place, London SW1W 9NF
and Basingstoke

Associated companies throughout the world

ISBN 0-330-34350 5

Copyright © Robin Cross 1996

The right of Robin Cross to be identified as the
author of this work has been asserted by him in accordance
with the Copyright, Designs and Patents Act 1988.

9 8 7 6 5 4 3 2 1

A CIP catalogue record for this book is available from
the British Library

Typeset by CentraCet Limited, Cambridge
Printed in Great Britain by
Mackays of Chatham plc, Chatham, Kent

Contents

Introduction

This book is based on a column I once wrote for the *Sunday Express*. It took me to the unlikeliest corners of London in search of the unexpected aspects of this great city – from castles in suburban Kingsbury to Romanesque sewage works in the wastelands of Beckton. I enjoyed silent communion with a 17th-century corpse in the bell tower of a beautiful Wren church in the City; tramped up the Strand to inspect the biggest teapot in the world; and tried my hand at an ancient form of skittles in the basement of a pub in Hampstead.

London is so old, so big and so overlaid with layer after layer of history that a book of this kind can only scratch the surface. Its aim, nevertheless, is to acquaint the inquisitive Londoner, or visitor to London, with some of the capital's more unusual features and in the process to throw a sideways light on its rich past and fascinating present. Sutton House, in Hackney, provides the perfect example: a remarkable Tudor survival in the East End, where a brilliant restoration has preserved not only centuries-old graffiti but also a psychedelic mural painted when squatters occupied the building in the 1970s.

Many of the curiosities in this book can be enjoyed for nothing. All that is required is the ability to look around when you are out and about in the streets of London. Many of these small urban delights remain unknown to Londoners, who hurry on by, bent on their business, without giving them a second glance. Over two million people a year walk over Boris Anrep's extraordinary mosaics in the entrance to the National Gallery, blithely unaware that they are trampling over Greta Garbo, Bertrand Russell, Edith Sitwell, Augustus John and sundry other worthies. Few City workers slogging down Cornhill pause to look up at the gruesome devils perched over their heads next to the church of St Peter upon Cornhill; still fewer know why they are there. But you can find out in these pages.

Nearly all of the places and features detailed in this book, from private houses to public conveniences, are accessible to visitors, although prior application will sometimes be required. Visiting them will take the intrepid urban explorer all over the capital. Some, however, occur in convenient clusters, and pedestrians will be able to take them in during the course of an agreeable stroll. The Strand and Fleet Street contain some of the most intriguing items in Curious London. Enjoy them and learn a little about the men and women who built them, lived in them and, on occasion, were buried in them.

Robin Cross London 1995

ABBEY MILLS PUMPING STATION

Isolated in the industrial wastelands of Beckton is the Abbey Mills pumping station, an abiding reminder that the Victorian passion for extravagant architectural ornamentation extended even to the mucky business of dealing with London's sewage.

The pumping station was designed by the engineer Joseph Bazalgette, who in the mid-19th century provided the whole of London, north and south, with a properly planned main drainage system. Before Bazalgette undertook this heroic task the Thames had become an open sewer. It produced a stench so great that 1858 became the year of the 'Great Stink'. The smell from the river was so overpowering that the windows of the House of Commons were draped in curtains soaked in chloride of lime and members debated whether they should move upstream to Hampton Court.

When it was finished, Bazalgette's system of 1,300 miles of sewers was complemented by a network of pumping stations of romantic design. The most elaborate is the Abbey Mills station, still in operation, where six major sewage pipes converge before their contents are hastened on to the sewage treatment works at Beckton. The pumping station was disguised under a Slavic dome flanked by two slender Moorish towers, all of which invited comparison with one of the great Byzantine churches rather than a sewage works. The towers were originally capped with huge minaret-like embellishments, which can be seen in both contemporary illustrations and the immensely beautiful architectural drawings preserved at the station, but they appear to have been very quickly removed.

Imposing brass doors and richly decorative brickwork attest to Bazalgette's no-expenses-spared approach to his brief. From the outside the pumping station seems like the mansion of some great Victorian steel baron or railway king, although much of the ornate, almost overpowering, detail has been eroded by pollution from the chemical works which sprung up in the area between the wars. Sadly, the great towers were demolished in 1940, as it was suspected that they were being used by Luftwaffe bombers to navigate their way down the Thames to raid London's docklands. All that remains of them are the massive plinths on which they stood.

The superb iron work inside the building survives, as does the extraordinarily beautiful gallery which housed the great beams of the original pumping engines. Below the gallery, in the bowels of the building, is the huge, heavy cast iron pipe through which billions of gallons of sewage have passed since the day the pumping station began operations. It has a science fiction feeling about it, like some weird machine dreamed up by Jules Verne to tunnel its way through the earth. In another corner of the building is a massive set of electrical switching gear, dating from the 1920s and only now about to be replaced. It's the kind of infernal machinery with which Charlie Chaplin might have tangled in *Modern Times* or which Ming the Merciless might have menaced Earth controlled in a Flash Gordon epic.

Until the seventies, the station's extensive grounds were tended by a permanent gardener, and many of the staff lived on the site in handsome cottages designed by Bazalgette. Now the station's surrounds have a melancholy, neglected feel about them, the result of the parsimony of the present day. Nevertheless, Abbey Mills remains the Mecca of sewage engineers and historians who beat a path to its great brass doors to savour the lingering glory of an heroic age of engineering.

Abbey Mills pumping station is in Abbey Lane, E15.
Tube: West Ham.
The station is not open to the public but visits and tours can be arranged by appointment. Tel: 0181 534 6717

APOTHECARIES' HALL,
BLACKFRIARS LANE

You can step off narrow, winding Blackfriars Lane into the 17th century. The courtyard of Apothecaries' Hall, rebuilt after the Great Fire of London, is the only one of London's Livery Halls not to have been destroyed either wholly or in part since 1666. Apart from some minor modifications the premises exist unchanged today.

The Society of Apothecaries traces its origins back to the 12th century and the Company of Pepperers who dealt in spices imported from the Middle East. 'Apothecarius' in medieval Latin means 'store keeper', and the great medieval houses kept stores of spices and medicines which apothecaries prepared under the direction of physicians. By the middle of the 16th century the title of Apothecary was restricted to those concerned with the preparation and selling of substances for medical purposes.

The Society was granted a Charter in 1617 by James I, and a fine portrait of the king hangs in the Great Hall – reached by an impressive staircase – which can seat up to 150 diners. Next to the portrait is a bust of Gideon de Laune, James I's apothecary, a solemn bearded gentleman who found enough time away from his pestle and mortar to father 37 children. Around the Great Hall hang huge portraits of Masters of the Society, dressed in black for ceremonial occasions. As wall space in Apothecaries'

Hall is running out, present-day Masters now commission a miniature of themselves for posterity.

High on one of the walls in the Great Hall are
the banners flown from the Society's barges, which
would take its members and apprentices up-river to
the Chelsea Physic Garden (*see* p. 41). The barges
were last used at the time of Nelson's funeral, but
today no trace of them remains.

Next door in the Court Room, panelled with
heavy Irish oak, is a cartoon by Reynolds for a
portrait of the great anatomist John Hunter, who
bears a striking resemblance to the actor Ralph

Richardson at his most quizzical. The Hall houses a potrait of another John Hunter, who was one of John Keats' examiners when the poet was studying to be an apothecary. The second John Hunter is a dead ringer for comedian Bob Hope.

Less likely to raise a laugh is the collection of ancient leech jars next door in the Parlour. The leech was the *sine qua non* of 17th-century medicine – individual doctors would use millions of the little bleeders – and is still used today as an anti-coagulant measure in plastic surgery. The cabinets in this room also contain a large collection of drug jars and the pill tiles which apothecaries used as chopping boards when preparing medicines. In the library an ornate, gleaming fireman's helmet serves as a reminder of the days when Apothecaries' Hall had its own factory and private fire brigade. The old factory buildings were demolished in 1929 and new offices built on the site, although the old counting house was preserved complete, retaining an elegant link with the past.

Apothecaries' Hall remains very much a working building, and in the 1990s the Society examines in nine different subjects of postgraduate medicine.

Apothecaries' Hall is in Blackfriars Lane, EC4.
Tube: Blackfriars.
It is not normally open to the public, but visits for groups can be arranged. Tel: 0171 236 1189

BT TOWER

It's called the BT Tower now, but for anyone of a certain age the high-tech totem pole which has dominated the streets around Fitzroy Square since 1965 will always be the Post Office Tower, potent symbol of the sixties.

Opened to the public on 19 May 1966 by Postmaster General Anthony Wedgwood Benn (who hadn't yet metamorphosed into 'Tony Benn'), the 580-foot Tower was the determinedly phallic expression of Prime Minister Harold Wilson's white-hot technological revolution. Millions of visitors took the high-speed lifts to the viewing gallery (at a price of four shillings, or twenty pence in today's money) to gawp at London's rapidly changing skyline. On a clear day you couldn't see for ever, but at least all the way to Croydon. In the revolving restaurant the capital's movers and shakers could dine for about five pounds a head.

The Tower was an intrinsic part of the huge film set that 'Swinging London' briefly became in the late sixties. In the 1967 film *Smashing Time*, Rita Tushingham contrived to blow up the revolving restaurant during one of those wild parties which wound up films in those days. Four years later a real bomb exploded in the gents' washroom on the 31st floor. No one has ever claimed responsibility. The building was closed to the public, although the restaurant, run by Butlin's, staggered on until it too was closed in 1980.

Work on the Tower began in 1961. It cost two and a half million pounds to build – hardly enough to buy an international footballer these days – and was opened for operations by Harold Wilson on 8 October 1965. Supporting the Tower's 13,000-ton bulk is a massive concrete raft on which squats a sawn-off concrete pyramid. The rough wooden platform which surrounds the pyramid, and the constant noise of running water, suggest a scenario from another sixties' film, *The Curse of the Mummy's Tomb*.

High above, microwave technology holds sway. The Tower's 57 large horn- and dish-shaped microwave aerials carry TV programmes, news, live outside broadcasts, telephone conversations and computer data. All of Britain's TV broadcasters, including cable and satellite, depend on the Tower, which also uses satellite technology to send live and recorded TV material all over the world and receive it from other countries.

The Tower has now passed from ultra-modernity into the ranks of listed buildings. Inside, few traces of the sixties survive. The ground floor ticket office is used for storage. In the corner is the postbox for visitors' postcards home from Swinging London. The restaurant, which can still revolve through 360 degrees every 22 minutes, now presents a bland corporate face for BT functions. Its small kitchen must be the highest in London.

The BT Tower, which is on the corner of Cleveland

*Street and Maple Street W1, is no longer open to the
public, but can be admired from the outside.*
Tube: Goodge Street

BELSIZE PARK
DEEP SHELTER

Squatting next to Belsize Park Tube station is a
massive concrete drum, a cross between a giant Art
Deco wedding cake and a house designed by a
disciple of Le Corbusier. It is the shafthead to one
of London's largest underground lairs.

Beneath Haverstock Hill lies one of the eight
'deep level' shelters begun in the winter of 1940,
while the Blitz was raging, and finished in 1942.
Before 1939 the government had been reluctant to
build such shelters, fearing that in the event of war
they would harbour a troglodyte population living
permanently underground. Each of the deep shelters was built directly under a Tube station and
consisted of two parallel 1,200-foot tunnels divided
into an upper and lower level.

The shelter at Goodge Street became General
Eisenhower's bomb-proof headquarters. The rest
were to be used as 'citadels' for key government and
military personnel in the event of a German bom-
bardment of London with rockets carrying nuclear
or chemical warheads. A great sigh of relief went
up when the V-1s and V-2s arrived in 1944 armed

only with high-explosive. The public was allowed to use four of the shelters during the V-weapon campaign. Human waste, a tricky problem so deep underground, was piped up to sewer level by a compressed air system.

There were post-war plans to link the deep shelters in a new Tube expressway, but these were never realised. As the Cold War took a grip, tunnelling continued. The 'citadels' were reserved for use by the governemnt during widespread civil disorder or nuclear attack, but the development of the H-bomb made them obsolete as shelters. In the late 1970s several of the shelters, including Belsize Park, were turned over to private enterprise for archive storage. The thousands of iron bunks on which Londoners had snatched uneasy sleep in the winter of 1944 were broken up and recycled as low-security storage cages. The Cold War redoubts became the last resting place for company records.

Tube: Belsize Park

BETJEMAN'S MURAL

On the wall of a house in Cloth Fair, Smithfield, for many years the home of Sir John Betjeman, Poet Laureate and much-loved chronicler of suburban 'Metroland', is one of the most charming follies in the City of London.

Betjeman lived at No. 43 Cloth Fair, snug in the small maze of medieval alleys which grew up around the Priory of St Bartholomew. Today the area retains the layout and feel of 13th-century London, with its network of narrow passages which meet and separate every few yards.

To one side of No. 43, at No. 41, stands one of the few remaining houses in the City built before the Great Fire of London. The architects who occupied it grew tired of staring at the blank wall of No. 43, and commissioned – no one seems to quite know when – the artist B.D.L. Thomas to paint a window on it which gives passers by a glimpse of a delightful domestic scene. A ruddy-faced Victorian sailor is returning to the bosom of his family. His excited children fling themselves into his arms while an exotic songbird – a souvenir of a previous voyage, perhaps – wobbles unsteadily over their heads in its cage. A sampler in the corner reads, 'Footsteps in the Sands of Time Are Not Made by Sitting Down'. There are other *trompe-l'oeil* paintings in London, but this is the liveliest. Betjeman was inordinately proud of it.

Equally lively were the parties held in No. 41, at which guests were invited to scratch their signatures on the window panes. The windows in the panelled room which serves as the boardroom of the present occupants are crowded with the autographs of the great and the good – Lady Diana Cooper, Bernard Miles, Joyce Grenfell, R. A. 'Rab' Butler and J.B. Priestley. In typically fussy fashion, Monty signed himself 'Montgomery of Alamein', adding, lest we forget, FM for Field Marshal. Anyone with a sharp eye and an ability to read a reversed image can decipher Yehudi Menuhin's autograph on the panes by the building's front door.

The area around Cloth Fair, a rich mix of the domestic and commercial now almost lost to London, positively hums with history. Opposite Betjeman's Wine Bar, which occupies the ground floor of No. 43, is the graveyard of St Bartholomew the Great, built by Henry I's jester in 1123 and London's oldest church. The church's gatehouse looks out on to Smithfield Market, now restored to its original Victorian glory. It was at Smithfield (the 'smooth field' where medieval jousts were held) that in 1381 the Lord Mayor of London, William Walworth, fatally stabbed Wat Tyler, the leader of the Peasant's Revolt. Tyler was hurried round the corner to St Bartholomew's Hospital (also founded in 1123), pursued by Walworth and his henchmen who dragged him out and beheaded him on the spot. The dagger which killed Tyler is kept at Fishmonger's Hall in King William Street – Walworth was a Fishmonger – and can be seen by appointment.

Betjeman's mural is at 43 Cloth Fair, EC1.
Tube: Barbican

BLACK FRIAR PUB

A French saying of the Middle Ages runs: 'To drink like a capuchin is to drink poorly. To drink like a Benedictine is to drink deeply. To drink like a Dominican is pot after pot. But to drink like a Franciscan is to drink the cellar dry'.

Patrons of the Black Friar pub, opposite Black-friars Station, can sink pot after pot in the company of several dozen of the most agreeable Dominican topers you will ever meet outside a monastery's walls. They form part of the extravagant décor which makes the Black Friar the only Art Nouveau pub in London.

Stranded on the edge of the fume-ridden race-track of Queen Victoria Street, the wedge-shaped pub no longer nestles in the warren of ancient streets which dictated its shape. Nevertheless, it stands as a reminder of the area's monastic past. The Black Friar was built on the site of a medieval Dominican Friary, where the 'Black Parliament' sat in the 15th century and where Henry VIII dissolved his marriage to Catherine of Aragon before pro-ceeeding to dissolve the monasteries.

The construction of the Black Friar began in 1875, but it was not until 30 years later, after a refurbishment by its architect, H. Fuller Clark, that the pub attained its full glory. The façade is domi-nated by a hugely jovial friar and lively mosaics by Henry Poole reminiscent of a Book of Hours. Below the mosaics Poole carved a jostle of bibulous monks

fighting to get into the bar. One of them has clearly given up and is refreshing himself under a tree with a bottle of wine.

Inside, Clark and Poole combined the voluptuous curves of Art Nouveau with the more homely medievalism of the Arts and Crafts movement. Sunlight filters through a stained-glass window on to bronze bas-reliefs of well-fed monks contemplating the delights of table or honking their krumhorns merrily in a rustic choir. The 'grotto' next to the bar is an extraordinary combination of cloister and Kardomah, clad with matched Italian marble and topped with a Romanesque mosaic ceiling in gold leaf. Pagan figures perch in the corners, swinging their legs mischievously in space. Amid the riot of detail in the grotto are delicate carvings of Aesop's fables and traditional nursery rhymes.

Customers are surrounded by improving inscriptions, picked out in handsome copper letters: 'Finery is Foolery' or 'Contentment Passes Riches'. Next to 'A Good Thing is Soon Snatched Up', a monk drains a colossal beaker of ale.

The cost of decorating the Black Friar bankrupted the original tenant, one William Petit, but he left us all the richer for it. On a quiet morning, before the lunchtime rush begins, the Black Friar is an excellent place to acquire a drinking habit.

The Black Friar is at 174 Queen Street, EC4
Tube: Blackfriars

BORIS ANREP'S MOSAICS, NATIONAL GALLERY

In her lifetime the reclusive Greta Garbo was celebrated for her famous cry, 'I want to be alone!'. She is never alone at the National Gallery, where every year over two million people hurry over her beautiful face, nearly all of them blissfully unaware that they are trampling on a famous film star.

Garbo forms just one of the details in a remarkable mosaic laid in the entrance of the National Gallery between 1938 and 1952 by the emigré Russian artist Boris Anrep and paid for by private patrons. The subject of the mosaic is nothing less than the intellectual life of the modern world, although Anrep adopted a distinctly quirky approach to this daunting artistic challenge.

There are four large mosaics in all. The first, in the west vestibule, illustrates the Labours of Life, showing the constructive and creative side of mankind. It is balanced in the east vestibule by the Pleasures of Life. The halfway landing connecting these two pavements depicts the Awakening of the Muses, while the mosaic in the north vestibule is devoted to the Moral Virtues.

Adorning the Awakening of the Muses is a serviceable likeness of Greta Garbo as the Muse of Tragedy. Virginia Woolf appears in this mosaic as the Muse of History, and Clive Bell turns up in jovial mood as Bacchus, the God of Wine. Lydia Lopokova, the wife of the economist John Maynard Keynes, is depicted as the Muse of Dance.

The mosaics form a fascinating gallery of the great and good of the thirties and forties. As the Moral Virtue of Defiance, a tin-hatted and boiler-suited Winston Churchill defies a Nazi dragon. Leisure takes the unlikely form of a studious T.S. Eliot contemplating the formula $E = mc^2$ and the Loch Ness monster. As Sixth Sense, Dame Edith Sitwell, reading a book of poems, crosses a chasm oblivious to menacing beasts and a predatory raven. Lucidity, the philosopher Bertrand Russell, awakens the comely naked figure of Truth and reaches out to remove her mask. Neptune, a whiskery Augustus John, rises from the waves to offer Alice in Wonderland gifts from the Sea. The great society beauty

Lady Diana Cooper appears as Humour, holding a copy of *Who's Who* and sharing space with a libidinous Mr Punch. The figure of Compromise looks a bit like Joan Collins in demented Dynasty mode, but is in fact a movie star from an earlier era, Loretta Young wearing a Phrygian cap and pouring red and white wine into a large cup. As Pursuit, the bespectacled young astronomer Fred Hoyle, looking the spitting image of silent comedian Harold Lloyd, shins up a church spire.

One of the Pleasures of Life includes Profane Love, in which a handsome young man contemplates his face in a mirror while being caressed by his girlfriend. A *menage à trois* is completed by their companion, a mannish young woman with cropped hair, a long cigarette holder and a lap dog. This mild decadence is balanced by the healthy pleasures of Cricket – not one of the Pleasures of Life in Anrep's native Russia – in which a wicket keeper reaches for a snicked ball.

Anrep could not resist the temptation to keep himself out of the pageant, and his self-portrait appears in a mocking reference to his tomb, with the legend 'Here I Lie' and a family crest of hammer and chisel.

The National Gallery is in Trafalgar Square, WC2
Tube: Charing Cross

BROMPTON ORATORY'S
DEAD LETTER BOX

London has long been a city where secret agents have plied their trade. From the days of the Elizabethan playwright/spy Kit Marlowe to the more recent activities of the KGB, the capital has been at the centre of the world of espionage.

There could be few more respectable locations than Brompton Oratory in Knightsbridge, but this splendid Catholic Church on the Brompton Road was the site chosen by the KGB as one of their safest dead letter boxes in London. It was here that documents or microfilm were left by one agent to be picked up by another.

The KGB's instructions were quite precise. 'As you face the church from the street the entrance will be on the right hand side. Go into the church. Just to the right of the entrance is an altar. It is a memorial to Englishmen who were killed in the war and has a copy of Michelangelo's famous statue Pietà – the dead Christ in his mother's arms. On the floor below the statue are the words "Consummatum est". Just to the left of the altar as you face it, are two large marble columns which are part of the architecture of the church. Both are very close to the wall. The DLB (dead letter box) site is behind the column nearest to the wall (if you are facing them, it is the right-hand column) in a little space between the actual column and the wall.'

These directions were sent by Moscow Centre to

its top people in London in April 1985, but were
almost simultaneously passed to British intelligence
by the double agent Oleg Gordievsky. The KGB's
confidence about the security of the Brompton
Oratory DLB seems somewhat misplaced: a visitor
might suddenly have entered the chapel to disturb
the retrieval of material; the probing hands of a
child might easily have found the packet of microfilm behind the column.

Nearby is another of the KGB's dead letter
boxes. Follow the path of lime trees along Cottage
Place to Holy Trinity Church. To the left of the
church is a statue of St Francis of Assisi. The KGB's
instructions ran: 'The statue is surrounded by a
small fence to protect the flowers planted around it.
If you stand facing the statue, there is a large tree
growing just to the left. The fence passes close to
the tree. The site for the DLB is on the ground at
the base of the tree, between the tree and the fence'.

Again, intelligence experts have pointed out the
risky nature of the site. Windows overlook the place
from the church and from nearby houses. Presum-
ably the KGB used these sites but we do not know
what use British intelligence made of their knowl-
edge of them. Within months Gordievsky had
defected and KGB operations in London were
reduced to a shambles. Brompton Oratory no longer
plays host to packets of microfilm.

Brompton Oratory is in the Brompton Road, SW1
Tube: Knightsbridge and South Kensington

BUNHILL FIELDS,
CITY ROAD

One of London's most fascinating burial grounds is
to be found in Bunhill Fields on the City Road. Its
name is probably derived from 'Bone Hill'. During
the Great Plague of 1664/5, which carried away
nearly 100,000 Londoners and raised a heavy, sweet
smell of putrefaction over the city, the Corporation
of London decided to use Bunhill Fields as a burial
ground. A brick wall was raised around it, but no
plague victims were ever buried there. Instead,
having never been consecrated, it became a favoured
resting place for Nonconformists, who could be
buried there without recourse being made to the
Book of Common Prayer. Eventually it became
known as the 'Cemetery of Puritan England'.

The last burial in Bunhill Fields took place in
1854, and it is now maintained for the use of the
public. In the shade of its stately plane trees, one
can enjoy a quiet lunch-time break, inspect the
spiked gate erected in the north-east corner to foil
grave robbers, and admire the monuments raised to
Daniel Defoe (who chronicled the Great Plague in
A Journal of the Plague Year), William Blake, John
Bunyan, the hymn writer Dr Isaac Watts, and Dame
Mary Page, whose tomb contains one of the saddest
of all epitaphs. The poor woman, the widow of Sir
Gregory Page, died in March 1728, a martyr to
dropsy. The epitaph records: 'In 67 months she was
tap'd [tapped] 66 times. Had Taken Away 240

Gallons of Water, Without Ever Repining at Her Care or Ever Fearing the Operation'.

John Wesley's mother, Susannah, is buried in Bunhill Fields. Nearby, on the other side of the City Road, Wesley himself is buried, in a grave behind the Chapel whose foundation stone he laid in 1777. Here, on a site reclaimed from swampland by soil dumped from the excavations for St Pauls' Cathedral, was raised the mother-church of Methodism, handsomely restored in the 1970s. Next door, at No. 47 City Road, is Wesley's London home, a shrine to Wesleyana open to the public. On the side of the house a series of tablets commemorates former ministers of the chapel, one of them the fearsomely named Edmund Grindrod.

Bunhill Fields is on the City Road, EC1
Tube: Old Street

BURTON'S TOMB, MORTLAKE

The woman who built it, Lady Isabel Burton, described it as 'by far the most beautiful, most romantic, most undeathlike resting place in the whole wide world'. Lurking in the brambly recesses of the Catholic Church of Mary Magdalene in Mortlake is the remarkable tomb she designed for her husband, the great Victorian adventurer Sir Richard Burton.

It has been said of Burton that no man can do all things at once, but no one tried harder to than this soldier, swordsman, poet, linguist, zoologist, botanist and explorer. Burton once observed that 'Discovery is mostly my mania', whether it was the forbidden Muslim cities of Medina and Mecca or the sexual secrets of erotic Eastern literature. Henry Morton Stanley said of him, 'What a great man! One of the real great ones of England, he might have been, if he had not been cursed with cynicism'.

Burton died in Trieste in 1860, his fiercely Catholic wife having engineered a dubious death-bed conversion. She was determined that her husband should lie alongside Livingstone in Westminster Abbey, but was told by the Dean, alarmed at the prospect, that 'there was no more room'.

Thus Burton came to be buried in the Catholic church in Mortlake, where he and Isabel had long owned a plot. He had once told her that, in death, 'I should like us both to lie in a tent, side by side'. He got his wish. His tomb takes the form of an Arab tent 18-foot high and 12-foot square, built from Forest of Dean stone, whose sides are sculpted to create the illusion of canvas tugged by a desert wind. Beneath the roof runs a frieze of Islamic stars and crescents, making an odd contrast with the crucified Christ over the door.

Burton's Catholic funeral created something of a furore. Only one member of his family attended, and the poet Swinburne, who hero-worshipped

Burton, wrote of the 'vulturous acclamation' with which the Catholic Church greeted Burton's conversion. Nevertheless, about 800 people turned up, many of them out of curiosity.

For the rest of her life Lady Burton visited the tomb every Sunday and bought a small cottage nearby to ease the rigours of her pilgrimage. The story goes that she held a number of seances in the stone tent, hoping, no doubt, that a man who had penetrated so many holy places and successfully returned would find some way back to her after death. Had he done so, Burton might have had some sharp words to say about Isabel's burning of the greater part of his papers and the weird, rambling account she wrote of their life together.

Originally, the tomb boasted a stained glass window at the back, but this has long since disappeared to be replaced by plate glass. Climb the iron ladder embedded in the rear wall and you can peer down into the last resting place of the Burtons, Isabel having joined her husband in 1869. Beneath the peeling, painted walls lie two coffins, one simple, the other ornate and gilded. Funerary bric-à-brac litters the floor and rusting camel bells dangle from the roof supports. Almost hidden under one of the coffins are photographs of the couple taken at the time of their marriage. The images look like one of the plates from Byron Farwell's biography of Burton, published 30 years ago, and left behind, perhaps, by a visitor to one of the strangest tombs in London.

*St Mary Magdalene is in North Worple Way, SW14
Railway: Mortlake*

CARDINAL WOLSEY'S
WINE CELLAR

Today there is little left of Henry VIII's great palace
at Whitehall. Cardinal Thomas Wolsey, the King's
Chancellor for many years, knew it as York House,
the London seat of the Archbishops of York before
Henry confiscated it in 1530 when Wolsey fell from
grace.

Henry, who amassed 14 palaces in the London
area and another 28 within easy reach of London,
was always a man to think big. He expanded
Whitehall to embrace all the land between Westminster and Charing Cross. The grounds were
planted with gardens and orchards, then embel-
lished with a tilting-yard (for tournaments and bear-
baiting), tennis courts and a cock pit. As the public
thoroughfare of Whitehall cut the Palace grounds in
two, Henry linked the two halves with a bridge
which came to be known as Holbein Gate after his
court artist Hans Holbein, who may later have
lodged in rooms over it. The gate was demolished
in 1759, but a wall that belonged to Henry's two
tennis courts survives behind the 19th-century 'Old
Treasury Building', which is now the Cabinet
Office.

Henry issued a set of strict rules governing the behaviour of those who lived in the Palace, enjoining them to be 'loving together, of good unity and accord', somewhat ironic considering his own troubled marital history. Whitehall dwellers were also to avoid all 'grudging, rumbling or talking of the King's pastime', not too difficult, perhaps, when one considers the King's wayward way with the axe.

A more solid survival of Henry's Palace is part of his wine cellar, which now lies under the Ministry of Defence main building on Horseguards Avenue, SW1. It was built by Cardinal Wolsey, but the poor man had little time to savour its contents before Henry dispensed with his services. The wine cellar was threatened with destruction in the late–1940s when the site was being redeveloped. To save it, engineers jacked up the vaulted brick-built cellar and moved it sideways on rollers until a new, deeper basement was built. The entire 800-ton structure was then moved back to its original position and lowered about 20 feet to its new level, with hardly a brick out of place.

In 1698 a careless Dutch laundry-woman started a fire which burned the old Palace to the ground, but the wine cellar remains to remind us of the rollicking days of King Hal.

Wolsey's Wine Cellar is beneath Horseguards Avenue, SW1. It is not open to the public, but an application to see it may be made to the Ministry of Defence.
Tel: 0171 218 2661.

Curious London

CAT MUSEUM,
HARROW-ON-THE-HILL

In the basement of Kathleen Mann's antiques shop in the High Street, Harrow-on-the-Hill, is a sight to set cat-lovers purring with delight. A trip down the stairs takes you into the world's only museum dedicated to cats.

Crammed into the room are over 300 cats of every shape, size and material. Jostling for space alongside prints and original drawings by Louis Wain are cat teapots, nut-crackers, scarecrows, toasting forks and thimbles – even a handsome bronze moggie that was cast, somewhat curiously, to mark the 100th performance of *Charley's Aunt* in Boston in 1894.

Kathleen's collection reflects the love affair people world-wide conduct with cats. One of her most unusual exhibits is a cat-shaped porcelain pillow from Korea, a distinctly uncomfortable-looking resting place for anyone's head. With its self-satisfied expression and neat black moustache, the 'pillow cat' bears a striking resemblance to left-wing Labour MP Ken Livingstone.

Kathleen is particulary fond of a John Petit print dating from 1789 and entitled 'A Procession of Old Maids at a Cat's Funeral'. A line of distraught spinsters in varying states of decrepitude makes its way to the grave, each of the maids clutching her pet. At the head of the procession the chief mourner bears a miniature coffin. Another favourite is a small

19th-century bronze of two cats playing billiards. One wall is dominated by a series of striking calendar prints showing elegant turn-of-the-century society women fondling an assortment of equally pampered feline friends.

The collection began over 20 years ago when Kathleen bought half a dozen cat items, including two English earthenware cats dating from about 1850. As the size of her collection swelled, the logical move was to create her unique museum. Kathleen explains, 'I had cats all over my flat collecting dust and people kept urging me to show them the collection, so I decided to put them all in one room and let everyone see them'.

Kathleen has had visitors from as far afield as Russia and Brazil. She runs the museum single-handed, with a little help from her own black and white cat Sophie, whom she refers to as 'my unofficial curator'. As you leave, the eye is drawn to a faded sampler dating from 1820 and bearing the legend 'Jane Jones Her Work'. On closer examination eight cats emerge from the background like the images in a puzzle painting, bidding the visitor a fond feline farewell.

The Cat Museum is at 49 High Street,
Harrow-on-the-Hill
Tube: Harrow-on-the-Hill.
The museum is open Thursday to Saturday from 9.30
a.m. to 5 p.m. and on Sunday from 2 p.m. to 5 p.m.
Tel: 0181 422 1892

CATO STREET CONSPIRACY

Today Cato Street, off the Edgware Road, is a quiet area of smart town houses. In the 1820s it was a very different place, an alleyway laid out with mean houses and mews. And on 23 February 1823 it wasn't at all quiet.

In the stable loft of No. 6 Cato Street (now No. 1A) a desperate band of 16 men had gathered to plot the murder of the entire Cabinet as it dined with Lord Harrowby in Grosvenor Square. They had already drawn up their plans in some detail. After murdering His Majesty's Ministers, the heads of Lord Sidmouth and Lord Castlereagh were to be cut off and taken away in a bag. Coutt's Bank in the Strand, which held the Royal accounts, was to be seized, as were the cannon in the Artillery Ground. Gray's Inn, the Mansion House and the Bank of England were to be captured, numerous other London landmarks put to the torch and a provisional government proclaimed. Not bad for a night's work.

The conspirators' plans were well known to the government who had a man on the inside. On the outside that night was a detachment of Coldstream Guards reinforced by Bow Street Runners. When they burst into the loft, the conspirators' ringleader Arthur Thistlewood, a much-travelled ex-soldier and estate agent who had drunk deeply of the revolutionary waters in America and France, ran through one of the Bow Street Runners with his sword. Several of the conspirators were seized, bundled into waiting cabs and rushed to Bow Street, but in the confusion 11 made good their escape.

On 1 May, Thistlewood and four others were hanged at Newgate but because of public sympathy for them were spared the indignity of being drawn and quartered. Nevertheless their heads were severed by a surgeon's knife, the last 'beheading' in British judicial history. The mob attacked the hangman in the street and nearly castrated him. Five other conspirators were transported to Australia, and the rest vanished, never to be heard of again.

In 1827, Cato Street became Horace Street (all the streets in the area have classical names), but 100 years later, when republican fires had long since dimmed, it reverted to its original name. The loft where the conspiracy was nipped in the bud remains, with a blue plaque to remind passers-by of what might have been one of the most blood-splattered nights in British political history. Nowadays estate agents make a different kind of killing in Cato Street.

Tube: Edgware Road

CHALK FARM
RAILWAY VAULTS

In 1994 the property arm of Railtrack announced the uncovering of a remarkable relic from the pioneering era of railways which had lain flooded and forgotten for 150 years.

Revealed now for the first time since the 1840s are the massive vaults built in 1837 by Robert Stephenson, chief engineer of the London and Birmingham Railway, to enable Euston to become London's first rail passenger terminus. They lie beneath the railtracks alongside the Camden goods yard in north London, only 200 yards from another symbol of the age of steam, the Round House engine shed.

A wire fence on the edge of the site, entered by a narrow spiral staircase, marks the boundary of a big new supermarket development. Hypermarkets may well be the cathedrals of our consumer society, but in Stephenson's day the great structures associated with the railways sang hymns to the unstoppable onward rush of technology.

Stephenson was in the vanguard. The only son of the original Rocket Man, George Stephenson, he was an engineer in the heroic Victorian mould, ready to contemplate the impossible and then achieve it. Long-span railway bridges were his meat and drink, the most famous example being the Britannia Bridge over the Menai Strait in north Wales.

The Chalk Farm vaults were an underground solution to a different kind of problem. They were built to house the steam-powered winches which hauled trains up the slope from Euston to Chalk Farm, as the locomotives of the day were not powerful enough to tackle the incline under their own steam. The continuous rope which pulled them was 10,000-foot long, seven inches in diameter and weighed twelve tons. Trains were tugged up the slope at 20 m.p.h. In a book published at the time, the engagingly titled *Stokers and Pokers*, Sir Francis Head recalled 'the moaning of the whistle signal from Camden followed by the loud ringing of the station bell, at which all the waiting cab horses raised their drooping heads and pricked their ears'.

When the engine room was completed, all that could be seen of it were two slim 132-foot exhaust chimneys rising above the busy 30-acre goods yard. Above ground were the yard's cattle pens, warehouses, coal yards and coke ovens. Down below, in the engine room, gangs of men stoked and tended the machinery as if they were in the innards of a great liner. The winching operation was co-ordinated by railway officials using what is believed to be Britain's first commercial electric telegraph. Running past the engine galleries was a tunnel connecting the goods yard to stables in nearby Gloucester Avenue, through which workhorses were led every day. Underneath the vaults, and in use until fairly recently, is another tunnel along which empty carriages could be run off from Euston to sidings.

The vaults, a great brick cavern 100-foot long and 63-foot wide, bear eloquent testimony to the skills of the Victorian engineers. They are almost cathedral-like in scale, and the bricks still 'work' and tremble as trains rumble overhead. Sadly, however, the vaults quickly outlived their usefulness. By 1844 locomotives could get up from Euston without the assistance of the winch. The great engines ground to a halt and were sold to a silver mine in Russia. The vaults were abandoned. They had been operating for so short a time that they do not appear on Ordnance Survey maps of the area. Nevertheless, they have survived both the death of steam and the axe that Dr Beeching took to the railway system which had been one of the glories of Victorian Britain. Now they await a new lease of life as a health centre, heritage gallery and shopping mall. The noise of rail traffic may soon be accompanied by the grunts of fitness fanatics going for the burn. According to English Heritage, 'The majestic scale of the vaults puts them in a class with other celebrated engineering monuments of the railway age. If treated sympathetically, there is no reason why they should not become known as one of the rediscovered sites of London.'

The vaults are not open to the public, but further
information is available from the property division
of Railtrack
Tube: Chalk Farm

CHARITY CHILDREN

In the days before universal state education, the children of the poor – if they were lucky – attended schools run by charities or the Church. Many of these charity schools can still be identified by the delightful figures of young girls and boys which decorate their facades.

Some were carved from wood but many were fashioned from a curious material called Coade stone. An artificial stone, and the most weatherproof ever made, it was used in the 18th century for statues and the decoration of many London buildings. At the Coade stone factory in Lambeth in the 1760s, Charity Children were made for 16 guineas per pair.

And very charming they are too, clutching their prayer books, the girls bodiced and bonnetted and the boys with smiling morning faces as shiny as the big buckles on their shoes. On the wall behind St Mary Abbots Church in Kensington Church Street the two Charity Children gaze sweetly at each other like childhood sweethearts. Other sites where you can see Charity Children include St Andrew's Church, Holborn; St Botolph's Church Hall, Bishopsgate; St Mary's School, Rotherhithe; Vintner's Place, Upper Thames Street; and the Sir John Cass School, Aldgate. Sir John Cass (1666–1718) was a carpenter's son who became an immensely wealthy and influential merchant and benefactor of the City of London. He died in 1718 of a haemmorrhage while signing his will and the quill was stained with

blood. The children of the school he founded attend an annual service on the anniversary of his death wearing red feathers in his memory.

The secret of the Coade stone of which the Charity Children are made died with the closing of the Lambeth factory in 1840. Three years earlier the Coade Artificial Stone Manufactory had turned out one of its most famous statues, the 12-foot-high, 13-ton Coade Lion. Painted red, it was placed over the entrance arch to the Lion Brewery near Hungerford Bridge and became a celebrated feature of

London's riverside. After visiting London in 1893, Emile Zola' wrote: 'It amused me greatly, this British Lion waiting to wish me good morning'.

The Lion vanished a few years before the Brewery was demolished in 1949 but re-emerged in 1951 to form part of the decorations for the Festival of Britain. At the request of George VI it was then removed to adorn the entrance of Waterloo Station before finding a new home on its present site, on the southern side of Westminster Bridge, in 1966.

There are many interesting Coade stone features in London: among them the Tragedy and Comedy frieze on the Royal Opera House, Convent Garden; the eight large caryatids supporting the pavilions at the eastern end of St Pancras Church, Upper Woburn Place; the lion which stands outside the rugby football stadium at Twickenham; and caryatids which decorate the facade of Sir John Soane's Museum at 13 Lincoln's Inn Fields. (see p. 126)

CHARLTON HOUSE

Lying some way off the traditional tourist track, Charlton House is one of the finest examples of Jacobean architecture in Britain. It was long thought that Inigo Jones was the architect, but although signs of his handiwork are evident in the Orangery, which is now a public lavatory, the likely attribution is to John Thorpe.

Charlton House was built for Adam Newton, tutor to Prince Henry, the son of James I (see Prince Henry's Room, p. 124). Its most celebrated occupant was one William Langhorn, a former Governor of Madras, who purchased the house for his retirement. Langhorn was tormented by the fact that in spite of two marriages late in life he had failed to produce an heir. He seems to have carried his frustration beyond the grave into which he was lowered at the advanced age of 85, for his ghost is said to chase young women around the house. It has even been accused of rape. Other ghostly manifestations at Charlton House include a spot on the landing, formerly overlooked by a carved devil's head, where visitors have often complained of a sinister chill. Since 1925 Charlton House has been run by Greenwich Council as a community centre and library.

There is an interesting tale attached to the origins of nearby Hornfair Road. The right to hold the medieval 'Horn Fair' was said to have been granted to a local miller by King John after he had seduced the miller's wife while hunting in the area. The miller was granted all the land visible from Charlton to the bend of the river beyond Rotherhithe. The miller's neighbours, mightily amused by his luck, dubbed the river boundary of his property 'Cuckold's Point' and initiated a Horn Fair, horns being the symbol of a cuckolded husband. The fair was held on 18 October, St Luke's Day, the parish church in Charlton being then, as now, St Luke's.

The Saint is often depicted writing beside an ox and cow sporting prominent horns, which points to a more prosaic explanation of the Horn Fair's beginnings. The Horn Fair was last held in 1872. In Charles II's reign thousands of day-trippers would descend on Charlton for the fair dressed as kings, queens and cuckolded millers with horns on their heads.

Charlton House is in Charlton Park, off Hornfair Road, SE7.

CHELSEA CRUISE

Do you remember the 'chicken run' between snarling Dennis Hopper and James Dean in *Rebel Without a Cause,* or the sight of Ed 'Kookie' Byrnes hot-rodding his way through the TV series *77 Sunset Strip*?

On the last Saturday of every month memories of these moments of pure Americana are rekindled in Battersea Park by devotees of the Chelsea cruise. It's a celebration of car culture in which the owners of up to 1,000 hot-rods, classic American cars and motorbikes gather to gun their engines, slaver over superchargers and admire several miles of gleaming chrome in the unlikely setting of the tarmac near the Park's Peace Pagoda. (see p. 115)

There's little chance of peace when a rodder

decides to 'burn rubber' in his classic 1941 Willys hot-rod. In the heady early days of the cruise, the acrid stench produced by spinning rear wheels before the rodder roared off into a gap in the traffic was a feature of the cruise. In true *American Graffiti* style, a seemingly endless line of cruising metal clogged the Kings Road, bringing traffic to a halt for miles around. So much for the joys of the open road; the rodders rejoiced at the frenzy to which the local traffic police were driven by the cruise.

Now all this automotive anarchy is almost as distant a memory as 'Kookie' Byrnes' Brylcreemed quiff. The rodders have been confined to the park and the critical contemplation of each other's wheels. There's plenty to admire: 'Resto-Rods' which ape their 1950s ancestors in every detail and flaunt flamboyant paintwork that is the result of 30 coats with a thorough rub-down between each one; classics like the Dodge Charger, a dream in cream and lime-green with whitewall tyres and fins like a pterodactyl's wings – the perfect chariot in which to date Jayne Mansfield; and England's unique contributions to the world of hot-rodding, – the supercharged Ford Popular (a 40 h.p. post-war family runabout transformed into a ravening 500 h.p. beast), and the Austin A30 with a V-8 engine.

The word 'awesome' is never far from a rodder's lips, and it's a verdict which is hard to withold from American 'muscle' cars like the 1963 Pontiac GTO, whose virtues Ronnie and the Daytonas hymned so movingly in *Little GTO*. The bonnet of a 1979 Corvette, slumbering under the trees like a big cat, is like a long, savage sneer, snarling 'eat my dust, punk!' A warning to joy-riders who might be tempted to try one out for size – you won't get far on eight miles to the gallon.

Most of the rodders are 40-somethings hankering after a try-out in the Robert Mitchum role in a remake of the classic road movie *Thunder Road*, in which country backroads unreel in moonshining Mitchum's headlights as if in a dream. In Battersea Park the dreams are anchored in suburban reality, with the sudden blast of a revving engine providing a hint of what might have been.

The Chelsea cruise gathers at the eastern end
of Battersea Park's Carriage Drive North.
Railway: Queenstown Road

CHELSEA PHYSIC GARDEN

One of London's most beautiful 'secret gardens' lies behind the ancient brick wall that runs down Swan Walk to the Chelsea embankment.

The Chelsea Physic Garden was founded by the Society of Apothecaries in 1673 to promote the study of botany in relation to medicine, known then as 'physic', the old name for the healing arts. Members of this private garden and their apprentices, who were admitted after ringing a bell which still hangs on the wall in Swan Walk, were given botanical instruction and taught how to identify the plants used in compounding and selling medicines.

The garden was originally three and a half acres but grew to nearly four with the creation of the Embankment by the Victorian engineer Bazalgette. It was essential for the Apothecaries to have a riverside site with a barge-house so that their students could be conducted there from the City of London to what was then rural Chelsea. The barge-houses still exist, although they had to be repaired after bomb damage in the Second World War. The gates on the Embankment are decorated with a golden figure of Venus vanquishing the serpent of Disease, and topped by a reproduction of Durer's drawing of a rhinoceros.

Within ten years of its foundation the Physic Garden was considered of sufficient importance for Paul Hermann, Professor of Botany at Leiden University, to visit it. The visit was returned in 1683 by the garden's director, Isaac Watts, and seeds and plants were exchanged, beginning a mutual exchange with other botanic gardens throughout the world that has continued uninterrupted to this day. Amongst the plants brought back by Watts were four cedars of Lebanon. One of them survived until 1904 when, weakened by London pollution, it was felled.

The ubiquitous John Evelyn, diarist and author

of the famous *Sylva*, was particularly impressed by his visit to Chelsea, writing of the 'subterraneous heat conveyed by a stove' which warmed the conservatory, probably the first heated greenhouse in the world.

The future of the Garden was secured by Sir Hans Sloane, who had studied there during his early training as a physician. Sloane bought the Manor of Chelsea from Charles Cheyne in 1712 and became the owner of the Garden's freehold. In 1722 he granted a lease to the Society of Apothecaries at five pounds a year in perpetuity, 'on condition that it be for ever kept up and maintained by the Company as a physick garden'.

In the 1750s, under the direction of the great botanical horticulturist Philip Miller, author of *The Gardener's Dictionary*, Chelsea became the finest botanic garden in the world. Cotton seeds from the Garden were sent to America, where they founded the staple crop of the South. Quinine was grown here in Miller's day, and for many years its bark provided the only anti-malarial drug.

In 1773 the earliest rock garden in Britain was built in the Garden. Many tons of old building stone from the Tower of London provided a base to display a quantity of basaltic lava brought by Sir Joseph Banks from Mount Hecla in Iceland. An intriguing if somewhat unaesthetic feature of the Garden, the rock garden is now listed and retains its significance as an early attempt to grow plants in an ecological arrangement which is common in all botanic gardens today. Some of Banks' lava can still be seen.

A stroll along the gravelled paths in this sheltered spot, with its mild micro-climate, reveals a horticultural cornucopia. Nearly a third of the Garden is taken up with botanical order beds containing about 100 plant families. Along the western wall is the Historical Walk, which links the history of the Garden and the people and plants associated with it from 1673 to 1880. Of particular interest is the Thomas Moore fernery. Other striking features include a fine Mediterranean trio of trees: a 30ft high olive tree, the biggest in Britain; a well-balanced cork oak tree; and a prickly Kermes oak.

In the north-east corner is the herb and medicinal garden, testimony to Sir Hans Sloane's desire that the Apothecaries and 'their apprentices and others may the better distinguish good and useful plants from those that bear resemblance to them and yet are hurtful'. This garden of useful plants and poisons contains everything from classic culinary herbs like basil and tarragon to a perfumery border and a bed of poisons. In the latter you will find the Castor Oil Plant from whose seed coat the poison ricin is obtained. (This is the substance used by the KGB to kill the Bulgarian dissident Georgi Markov, who was jabbed by an impregnated umbrella point on Waterloo Bridge.) A more benign use of ricin is in the treatment of rheumatoid arthritis.

In the glasshouses, the steamy 'Rainforest Corridor' displays a sampling of medicinal plants of the tropical and temperate rainforests, increasingly important as a source of current and potential medicines. Among them you will find plants like 'The Vine of the Spirits' (*Banisteriopsis*) which the Huaroni shamans of the Ecuadorian Amazon use to make hallucinogenic journeys on which they assume the shape of their spiritual counterparts, jaguars, eagles and boas.

If you are fortunate you may see (and smell) the transient white flowers of *Alpha officinarum*, a relative of Ginger which the Arabs used as an aphrodisiac and which is still used in Asia for bronchial complaints. Several species of yam can be seen in the corridor. It was from the tubers of these climbing plants that contraceptives and other steroids were developed in the 1960s. In the small section which links the tropical and temperate corridors, you will find the Queensland Chestnut (*Castanospermum australe*), currently under clinical trial as an inhibitor of the AIDS virus.

In the shade of a mulberry tree is the Garden of World Medicine, where you will find plants used medicinally by a wide variety of peoples, from the North American Indians to the Maoris of New Zealand. The scientific past and future merge seamlessly in the Chelsea Physic Garden. On the wall of the Gardening School is the ferny-leaved *Sohora microphylla*, a form of New Zealand's national plant known there as 'Kowhai'. The Chelsea specimen is reputedly a grandchild of the original material Sir Joseph Banks brought back from Cook's first voyage in the *Endeavour*. It flowers well in April and seeds itself around.

In the summer months the profusion of growth at Chelsea, far from swamping the Garden's four acres, seems to swell its size and blur its rectilinear 17th-century plan. Gazing south across the river through the dreamy blue foliage of its Chinese Foxglove tree, you can see the golden tip of the Peace Pagoda in Battersea Park. In the centre of the garden, and surrounded by swimming colour, is a fibreglass replica of Rysbrack's statue of Sir Hans Sloane (the original being on loan to the British Museum), the great benefactor of a garden that not only retains its 300-year-old function as a centre of scientific research but also provides a peaceful haven for the keen gardener and casual visitor alike.

The Chelsea Physic Garden is at 66 Royal Hospital Road, SW3.
Tube: Sloane Square.
It is open from 2 p.m. to 6 p.m. Sunday and 2 p.m. to 5 p.m. Wednesday, April to October. Admission charge. Schools by appointment any time of the year, no charge. Tel: 0171 352 5646

CORNHILL DEVILS

Perched dizzily over the entrance to St Peter's Church in Cornhill are three terrifying figures, their

faces contorted with devilish rage. For all the world it looks as if they are about to swoop from their eyrie and tear some hapless City gent limb from limb.

On closer inspection it can be seen that the Cornhill Devils form no part of the church. They are, in fact, the legacy of a feud between the Church of England and the architect of the 19th-century office block which rubs shoulders with St Peter's.

The architect, one Rentz, had encroached on the church's land and was forced to redraw his plans. The gargoyles were his revenge. The face of the fiercest is said to resemble his arch-enemy, the rector of St Peter's.

After squinting at the gargoyles, the church is well worth a visit. It was allegedly founded on the site of a Roman basilica by Lucius, the first Christian king of Britain, in AD 179. In the Middle Ages it housed a large library and a grammar school. It was burned down in the Great Fire and rebuilt by Sir Christopher Wren in between 1677 and 1678. In the 1870s it was restored by J.D. Wyatt, who removed much of Wren's furniture. However, there still remain a wooden screen, an impressive pulpit with sounding board and the Father Smith organ on which Mendelssohn played in 1840 and 1842.

St Peter upon Cornhill, EC3.
Tube: Bank

DAVENPORTS
MAGIC SHOP

For collectors, connoisseurs and the merely curious, London's vast array of specialist shops is a source, of endless delight and one of the most attractive features of city life. Do you want a succulent

Bradenham ham? Then beat a path to the elegant door of Paxton & Whitfield, purveyors of hams and fine cheeses since 1797. People with a passion for stuffed animals will be enthralled by the amazing display of taxidermy at Get Stuffed on Islington's Essex Road. At J.P. Guivier & Co. in Mortimer Street, near Broadcasting House, music lovers can buy a do-it-yourself violin kit from China or a cello worth thousands of pounds. London has everything to excite the eye, soothe the ear and tickle the taste-buds.

Tucked away in a corner of the underground concourse at Charing Cross station is Davenports, the finest magic shop in the world. It was founded in 1898 by Lewis Davenport, a celebrated magician whose speciality was the lightning-fast manipulation of solid billiard balls. The shop remains in family hands and a fifth generation of Davenports continues to ply the founder's magical arts.

Over the years Davenports has assembled an intriguing private collection of magic items and literature, including a very early book on the subject, *The Discovery of Witchcraft*, which was published in 1584 and describes tricks thousands of years old. The assistants at Davenports oblige customers by demonstrating, but not explaining, the shop's range of tricks. Small children squeal with delight as they are shown the timeless pleasures of simple rope tricks like 'The Professor's Nightmare', which will set the would-be David Copperfield back a mere £2.

*Davenports is at No. 7 Charing Cross Underground
Shopping Arcade, the Strand, WC2
Tube: Charing Cross. Tel: 0171 836 0408*

DOME READING ROOM,
IMPERIAL WAR MUSEUM

When they glance up from the minutiae of 20th-
century military history, readers in the Imperial
War Museum's reference library are given a stern,
silent warning – 'Thou Shalt Do No Murder'.

The panel bearing the Ten Commandments
which has looked down on several generations of
military historians is a reminder that the library is
housed in a chapel. And one with a poignant past,
for its worshippers were the inmates of the Bethlam
Royal Hospital, or Bedlam as it was popularly
known.

At a time when the world is still racked by the
madness of war there is some irony in the fact that
since 1936 the Imperial War Museum's home has
been a former lunatic asylum. The great classical
pile in St George's Fields, Lambeth, was built in
the 19th century to replace the original, notorious
Bedlam in Moorfields, where the public had paid to
watch the cavortings of the wretches incarcerated
there. The regime at the new hospital was more
enlightened. Its 300 patients were drawn mainly

from the 'professional and educated classes'. Contemporary engravings show the less dangerous inmates wandering, polite and forlorn, in the seemingly interminable male and female recreational galleries in the hospital's upper storeys.

At the head of the grand staircase hung a large painting of the Good Samaritan by Richard Dadd, the brilliant, demented artist who was confined in the criminal wing after killing his father. In the southern wing there was a ballroom where monthly dances were held, prompting a writer in the *Illustrated Times* to reflect: 'Ah, those periodical balls at Bethlem Hospital – who can describe them, who can imagine them, with their strange and pervading characteristics and underlying peculiarities'.

The chapel sits at the very top of the building under an imposing dome. It's a pleasant octagonal, galleried room dominated by a huge chandelier which looms over the circular readers' desk. Here, in the days of Bedlam, 'Such of the patients as can be trusted to behave themselves attend service in it twice on a Sunday, the men sitting on one side and the women on the other, each attended by their keepers or attendants … the patient's themselves form a very fair choir. They have a good organ to aid them in their psalmody'.

Nowadays, the only noise to break the studious silence is the furious muted clacking of laptop computers and, on blustery days, the moaning of the wind around the dome.

The Imperial War Museum is on Lambeth Road, SE1.
Tube: Lambeth North.
The public can use the Imperial War Museum's
Library, for which admission is free, by appointment.
Tel: 0171 416 5000

DRUMMONDS BANK, TRAFALGAR SQUARE

Dealing with your High Street bank can be a dispirit-ing business. Struggle to the head of the queue and it's an even-money bet that the Next-suited youth behind the counter will immediately disappear for lunch. Take your bank manager out to dine and he will charge you handsomely for his time.

There is another way. Pass through the elegant doors of Drummonds Bank, tucked away in a corner of Trafalgar Square, and you step back into a more civilised age. Under the chandeliers of the banking hall the sombre ticking of antique clocks suggests a great house rather than the former family business which since 1924 has been known as Drummonds Branch, the Royal Bank of Scotland. Here you can still sign your cheques with goose quills perched in pewter inkwells under the gaze of Zoffany's benign portrait of Andrew Drummond, the Scottish gold-smith who came south to found the bank in 1712.

Less benign, perhaps, are the eight superbly crafted muskets housed in a cabinet near the entrance – reminders of the prudent measures that the partners took to protect themselves from the mob after the Gordon Riots of 1780. A Drummond family motto on a crest in the banking hall reminds customers to 'gang warily'.

Behind the scenes Drummonds has many treasures. In the old boardroom are lodged more than 500 massive customer ledgers from 1715 to 1945, a goldmine for researchers and historians. Notable former customers of Drummonds include Lord North, Spencer Perceval (the only British Prime Minister to be assassinated), Lord George Gordon (fermenter of the riots which so alarmed the partners), James McNeill Whistler and Beau Brummell, the great Regency dandy.

When Brummell opened his account at Drummonds in January 1800, he had an income of over 4,000 pounds per year. But at the end of 1815, a few months before he fled to France, his credit balance was only £18 7s 5d; his friends described him as 'wiped out clean'. Later, his brother paid in an annual allowance of 70 pounds, and at the end of 1835 – eight months after his imprisonment for debt and four years before his death in the madhouse at Caen – the account was finally closed with a pathetic overdraft of eight pence.

George III was also a customer, and a series of the mad monarch's signatures chart the deterioration of his health as his writing grows ever more spidery and dislocated.

Drummonds holds one more surprise, a cache of

prehistoric animal bones unearthed in the 1870s when the old bank building was demolished and the present premises erected. A bank is an unusual place to inspect the remains of a sabre-toothed tiger.

Drummonds is at 49 Charing Cross, WC2
Tube: Charing Cross

EDWARD WYNTER MEMORIAL, ST MARY'S BATTERSEA

The tomb of Edward Wynter contains one of the most grandiloquent epitaphs ever composed. It records that 'Alone unarm'd a Tigre he opprest/And crushed to death ye Monster of a Beast/Thrice-twenty mounted Moors he overthrew/Singly on foot, some wounded, some he slew/Dispers'd ye Rest. What more could Samson do'.

What indeed! Wynter was a man with something to prove. His brother had been a confederate of Guy Fawkes and had been executed for his part in the Gunpowder Plot of 1605. Edward was a merchant with the East India Company, but clearly no 'box wallah'. This ferocious crusher of Tigres and smiter of Moors retired in 1682 to Battersea, where he became a benefactor of St Mary's, which also possesses one of his silver chalices. Wynter died in 1685 at the age of 65. A street in the neighbourhood is named after him.

St Mary's is off Battersea Church Road, SW11
Railway: Clapham Junction

8 ADDISON ROAD,
HOLLAND PARK

Rearing its head above the trees near Holland Park
is one of the most remarkable private houses in
London, built in 1906 by the architect Halsey
Ricardo for department store king Sir Ernest
Debenham.

The house is a monument to the art of the tile-
maker. The exterior glistens with brilliant blue and
green glazed brickwork and cream Carrara ware.
The main entrance is guarded by a long Italianate
covered way which gleams from end to end with
peacock blue and dark green tiles, panels of flowers,
vases and stylised peacocks. They are the work of
William de Morgan, who also played a major part in
another fantastically decorated residence, nearby
Leighton House (see p. 92). A final flourish is
provided by Ricardo's name and the date of the
house on a panel of cypress and pomegranate trees
in a Tuscan landscape.

Spectacular as it is, nothing on the house's
exterior can prepare the visitor for the astonishing
first sight of Sir Ernest's Byzantine Hall. Walls of
turquoise blue tiles sweep up to marble balconies
under a dome rich with glittering mosaics designed

by Gaetano Meo and inspired by the churches of Ravenna. Amid signs of the zodiac and a small army of Greek gods, portraits of Sir Ernest and Lady Debenham and their eight children sit proudly in Meo's mosaic. The story goes that the children helped the artist create their own images with little bags of golden chippings.

The 'Peacock House', as it is sometimes known, was burnished by leading members of the Arts and Crafts movement. Richly worked brass, enamel and glass attest to their skills. And everywhere you look are de Morgan's vibrant tiles: in a bathroom owls pounce on hapless mice; peacocks stalk along the passages; and a bedroom fireplace boasts a entire fleet of lustre ships. Each of the 28 tiled fireplaces in the house has its own design. They are, to say the least, eclectic. Some of the tiles were originally intended for the Tsar's yacht, which had the misfortune to be torpedoed in the First World War; others were a commission for an ocean liner.

Sir Ernest was an aficionado of state-of-the-art domestic technology. The house's central vacuum system was powered by a huge motor in the basement, sucking in the dust from every nook and cranny. A telephone was connected to West End theatres so that the family and guests could enjoy live performances. During the Second World War the house escaped German bombs, although a 500-pounder came down in the extensive grounds, which pastured a herd of cows. The caretaker created a potato patch in the crater it made.

Over £50,000 were poured into the Peacock House, but by the mid-1960s, when it was taken over by the Richmond Fellowship, its Edwardian extravagance was considered so unfashionable that the remainder of the lease went for about one tenth of the building price. (Sir Ernest never managed to buy the land on which his creation stood.) It seems priceless now.

The Peacock House is at 8 Addison Road, W.14
Tube: Holland Park.
It is not open to the public but the Richmond
Fellowship organises occasional open days

THE ELECTRIC CINEMA, PORTOBELLO ROAD

Climb the narrow, creaking stairs to the projection room of the Electric Cinema and you are following the footsteps of a serial killer. One of the footnotes to the Electric's long and colourful history is the period during the Second World War when its projectionist was the necrophiliac John Reginald Halliday Christie, who was hanged for his crimes in Brixton Prison.

The Electric is one of the oldest purpose-built cinemas in London. Film buffs argue endlessly about its exact antiquity, but one source states that it opened for business on 27 February 1911 with a film of Sir Henry Beerbohm Tree's performance in Henry VIII at her Majesty's Theatre.

In those days the cinema was an upstart rival of music-hall and theatre, and the Electric's décor reflected its pretensions. The terracotta façade had *trompe-l'oeil* designs (never finished because the money ran out). The screen at the end of the barrel-vaulted interior was painted directly on to the wall and surrounded by a moulded proscenium arch, above which a large globe suggested the infant film industry's worldwide ambitions. Roof and wall panels were surrounded by decorative friezes and painted ribbons. Among the Electric's innovative safety measures was an enclosed projection room to protect the audience in the days of highly inflammable nitrate stock.

From the day it flung open its doors, the Electric rode the switchback of cinema history. During the First World War its patrons claimed that the manager, a man of German extraction, was signalling to Zeppelins from the roof. In the 1920s, renamed the Imperial, it fast became an anachronism, a flea pit existing in the shadow of the great Art Deco picture palaces rising in London. By the late 1950s, the Electric's audiences were being force-fed a film diet of old George Raft thrillers and Audie Murphy B-Westerns in which the only thing that ever changed was the horses. Rain leaked through the roof into strategically placed buckets, and whole rows of seating were liable to collapse if a customer sat at the wrong end. In the sixties comatose audiences watched scratchy old horror movies through a haze of marijuana fumes.

Thanks to the orginal lease, which stipulated that the building could be used only to show films, the cinema survived. It re-emerged as the Electric Cinema Club, temporarily equipped with projection equipment from Winston Churchill's private viewing theatre, and in 1972 a preservation order was granted.

The Electric is now managed by Electric Triangle Partners and is the only black-owned and run cinema in London. The original plasterwork and gilding have been elegantly restored by Simon Wedgwood, a descendant of the great Josiah Wedgwood. There are still Edwardian gas-fittings on the walls, but now the auditorium reverberates to a Dolby sound system rather than frenzied piano accompaniment to the on-screen action. The new screen partially obscures the globe above the proscenium arch, on which the continents are boldly picked out in gold.

The Electric's imaginative programme includes live events and the occasional re-run of the feature which captured the creepy Christie on celluloid, Richard Fleischer's *10 Rillington Place*.

The Electric is at 191 Portobello Road, W11
Tube: Notting Hill Gate and Ladbroke Grove.
Tel: 0171 792 2020

EPSTEIN'S MUTILATED STATUES
ON THE STRAND

Walk east up the Strand, past Charing Cross station, and at the corner of Agar Street you will find Zimbabwe House. Look up and you will see above you a frieze of 18 large figures, classical in form but sadly mutilated, with missing heads and arms. They are not the survivors of some ancient Greek site, borne back to London by a Victorian collector, but all that remains of the sculptor Sir Jacob Epstein's first large-scale commission. In 1908 these figures produced a furore every bit as lively as the recent rumpuses over the bricks in the Tate or Damien Hirst's sheep in a tank.

The 27-year-old Epstein had been commissioned by the British Medical Association to decorate its new headquarters. Rather than portray a collection of eminent whiskered surgeons, Epstein chose to sculpt 18 male and female nudes in their various stages from birth to old age.

Even before the scaffolding had come down, Epstein's figures attracted the attention of Scotland Yard. A policeman appeared on the scene and took copious notes. Peering over his shoulder, Epstein noticed the world 'rude'. No less a figure than the Bishop of Stepney, Dr Cosmo Gordon Lang, declared, after a close inspection, that there was nothing indecent about the figures. The *Evening Standard* begged to differ. On 19 June 1908 it announced its opposition to the sculptures being 'laid bare to the gaze of all classes, young and old, in perhaps the busiest thoroughfare of the Metropolis of the world'.

Battle was joined. Scotland Yard pursued its prurient inquiries and a sinister-sounding organisation called the National Vigilance Society entered the fray. As open-topped buses passed the building, the passengers would stand up *en masse* to catch a glimpse of the 'rude' sculptures.

To its credit, the BMA stood by Epstein, but the story did not have a happy ending. In 1935 the government of Southern Rhodesia bought the building and reopened the argument. Epstein called it the 'Thirty Years War'. By now frost and rain had removed some of the figures' offending appendages. Then a head fell off. The sculptures were declared a hazard to passers-by and were mutilated to prevent accidents.

Reflecting on the sorry history of the statues, Epstein observed: 'I had to discover for myself how superficial is the world of art, and what a wretched lot of log-rollers, schemers, sharks, opportunists, profiteers, snobs, parasites, sycophants, camp-followers, social climbers and . . . four flushers infest the world of art'. The same is probably true today.

Zimbabwe House is on the Strand, WC2
Tube: Charing Cross

FREUD MUSEUM, FINCHLEY

At 20 Maresfield Gardens, a peaceful tree-lined street a short walk from the Finchley Road, is a peculiarly English shrine to one of the great minds of the 20th century, Sigmund Freud.

Freud lived in this house from September 1938 to his death at the age of 83 on 23 September 1939. His daughter Anna, the only one of his children to follow Freud into psychoanalysis, lived here until her death in 1982. In accordance with her wishes the house is now a museum run by the Sigmund Freud Archives.

Freud came to London as a refugee from the Nazis. His works, and those of fellow psychoanalysts, were publicly burned in 1933, when the Nazis came to power in Germany. During the following years members of the predominantly Jewish psychoanalytical community in his native Vienna emigrated. Freud refused to be forced out, and it was not until Austria was annexed by Germany in 1938, and his family was subjected to Nazi harassment, that he left his home of 47 years, Bergasse 19.

On 6 June he arrived in London, and after a brief spell in a rented house at 39 Elsworthy Road, Freud moved into Maresfield Gardens, an airy, spacious house. Here his architect son Ernst and devoted housekeeper Paula Fichtl recreated for him his working environment exactly as it had been in Vienna.

Freud's study on the ground floor is a slice of
Vienna transplanted to north London. Everything
here came from Bergasse 19: the books, paintings,
and antiquities as well as Freud's original analytic
couch, covered with a rich Persian rug, on which
his patients would recline comfortably while Freud,
out of sight in a green tub chair, listened to their
'free association'. They were asked to say everything
that came to mind without consciously sifting or
selecting information, and this method became the
basis upon which psychoanalysis was built.

There is a depth to the quiet in this room which
is almost uncanny. It is saturated with antiquities
from ancient Greece, Rome, Egypt and the Orient,
which Freud collected obsessively. He confessed
that his passion for collecting was second in inten-
sity only to his addiction to cigars. The artefacts in
his study gave him both pleasure and food for
thought. He once explained to a patient that con-
scious material 'wears away' while what is uncon-
scious scarcely changes at all: 'I illustrated my
remarks by pointing to the antique objects about my
room. They were, in fact, I said, only objects found
in a tomb, and their burial had been their
preservation'.

When Freud sat down at his desk, he was faced
by serried ranks of Egyptian gods. Ancient faces
stare out from every cabinet, shelf and corner: a
strange little pot-bellied pre-Columbian fiqurine
with wide-awake eyes, said to be an official 'under
the influence of cocaine'; an Egyptian coffin mask of

the Roman period with burning obsidian eyes; a sphinx; lines of Etruscan stick men; Egyptians rowing a reed boat or pulling a plough.

Freud's pebble-lensed spectacles lie on the table next to copies of the laconic one-line diary he kept from 1929, when, stricken with cancer of the jaw caused by his beloved cigars, he was living on borrowed time. The first entry reads, '31 October Passed over for the Nobel Prize'. Five entries later, he notes anti-Semitic disturbances.

Upstairs, on the landing, are two interesting portraits of Freud. The first, by Salvador Dali, was made in 1938, after Dali had been introduced to Freud by Stefan Zweig. During this intriguing encounter between the interpreter and the painter of dreams – the inspiration of Terry Johnson's play *Hysteria* – Dali executed a sketch surreptitiously and later made the pen and ink drawing. Neither the sketch nor the drawing were shown to Freud because Zweig felt they conveyed Freud's imminent death.

The other portrait is by Ferdinand Schmutzer and shows Freud in the stern mode of popular imagination, fixing visitors with a penetrating and slightly unnerving gaze. However, another side of Freud is revealed in the museum's video compilation of home movies made of his household in the 1930s in Vienna and London. Narrated by Anna, they give him an endearing, domestic dimension, as he plays with his adored Chow dogs, is fussed over by the women in his family, and receives presents from children in a country garden on the anniversary of his golden wedding. The last we see of him, shortly before his death, is a brief smile and a retreating back as he disappears through the French windows at Maresfield Gardens, pursued by a small, yapping dog. At the end of the video is a rare recording of Freud's voice, made for the BBC. Speaking in excellent English, with only the barest trace of a central European accent, he describes the fierce resistance he encountered to his theories. He concludes, 'In the end we succeeded, but the struggle was not yet over'.

The Freud Museum is at 20 Maresfield Gardens, NW3 Tube: Finchley Road. Railway: North London line at Finchley Road and Frognal.
The Freud Museum is open from 12 p.m. to 5 p.m. Wednesday to Sunday (pre-booked tours at additional times by arrangement) Admission charge. Telephone: 0171 435 2002/5167

FULHAM PALACE

A 19th-century bishop called it a 'haven of ancient peace', and even today Fulham Palace remains one of London's best-kept secrets, casting a rural spell by the banks of the Thames near Putney Bridge.

Bishops have lived on the site since it was acquired by Bishop Waldhere in AD 704, but the

Church was a relative latecomer. Local archaeologists have uncovered evidence of Neolithic, Roman and Saxon settlements. The development of the present complex of buildings at Fulham Palace began early in the 13th century, and until 1973 they were the home of the Bishops of London. Now they are in the care of Fulham and Hammersmith Council, which since 1993 has opened parts of them to the public.

The Palace combines a range of architectural styles, ranging from mellow Tudor to severe Georgian and exuberant High Victorian. The oldest surviving part is the Tudor courtyard, with its diapered brickwork, 18th-century belltower and soothing Victorian fountain. Sitting here on a sunny day, the London explorer might be deep in the heart of Sussex or Kent rather than a mere four miles from Hyde Park Corner.

In the 18th century, when the old Palace had fallen into a sad state of disrepair, a programme of modernization was launched by the energetic Bishop Sherlock, a keen swimmer who was dubbed the 'plunging prelate' by the poet Alexander Pope. A few years later Bishop Terrick gave the Palace a 'Gothick' makeover, supervised by the splendidly named architect Stiff Leadbetter. Sadly, most of his extravagances were subsequently removed by the starchy Bishop Howley, and only an engraving of 1812 provides a nostalgic record of Terrick's fanciful incrustations. His towers and battlements have gone; only some pointed windows remain.

Another sad loss is the interior of the Chapel designed by William Butterfield in the 1860s. Butterfield's High Victorian symphony of elaborately patterned coloured bricks, marbles and encaustic tiles did not survive the austere post-war regime of Bishop Wand, who had them painted over. Wand also commissioned a decidedly odd set of murals by Brian Thomas, in one panel of which a contemporary young couple, supposedly modelled on Princess Elizabeth and Prince Philip, kneel beneath the Cross in prayer and sport outfits that might have come from a 1947 Simpson's countrywear catalogue.

The Palace grounds are a revelation. Once enclosed by the longest moat in England, the original 36 acres have been reduced to 13. The gardens earned early fame in the 17th century, when Bishop Compton imported rare species such as the magnolia and cultivated them for the first time. Today's grounds are graced by majestic oaks and cedars of Lebanon, extensive botanic beds, a herb garden and a wisteria pergola within the grassy expanse of the old walled garden.

The Palace boasts a charming museum housed in Bishop Howley's Dining Room and Bishop Porteus' Library. There are also organised tours of the grounds and some of the Palace's principal features, including the Great Hall, where in the reign of the Catholic Queen Mary the bloodthirsty Bishop Bonner is said to have tortured hapless Protestants. His ghost haunts the rooms overlooking the courtyard.

Fulham Palace is on Bishop's Avenue, SW6
Tube: Putney Bridge. Railway: Putney.
From March to October it is open from Wednesday to
Sunday, 2–5 p.m. November to February from
Thursday to Sunday, 1–4 p.m. Also open on Monday
Bank Holidays. Admission charge to museum. Grounds
open daily. Tel: 0171 736 3223

GAUMONT STATE, KILBURN

Sandwiched between the Bellavista Restaurant and a boarded-up shop on a fly-blown stretch of the Kilburn High Road is a towering monument to the golden age of British cinema-going, the Gaumont State.

When it was built in 1937, the Gaumont State's proud boast was that it was the largest cinema in the world, capable of seating 4,000 film fans. Its main feature, from which it derived its name, was an impressive 137-foot tower loosely modelled on the Empire State Building in New York. Originally flood-lit at night and topped by a huge revolving letter 'S', the tower is a masterpiece of Art Deco commercial, waiting in vain to play host to a British version of the rampaging King Kong.

Designed by George Coles, the leading cinema architect of the day, the Gaumont State cost £350,000 to build, ten times the cost of most cinemas of the time. It was a luxury ocean liner of the movie world, leaving rusty little tubs like Notting Hill's Electric (see p. 57) wallowing in its wake. The *Willesden Monthly Illustrated* reported on its opening with breathless excitement: 'Its dimensions and magnificence are almost breathtaking. On either side of the entrance hall are black-marble and gold-ornamented pillars, pink mirrors, several candelabras and a replica of the electrical fitting as in the Ballroom at Buckingham Palace'.

The royal connection did not stop there. On 20 December 1937 Queen Mary was the guest of honour at the Gaumont State's gala opening. She had stiff competition from the Band of the Grenadier Guards, Henry Hall and his Orchestra and Gracie Fields, the biggest domestic star of the day.

The Gaumont State's patrons were guaranteed value for money. The films were supported by variety shows. A signed playbill of 2 May 1938 lists no fewer than 40 acts, including the harmonica king Larry Adler, former boxing champion Bombardier Billy Wells, and Graham Moffat, the famous fat boy of Will Hay's comedy films. There were six projectors, a stage the size of four houses, a mighty Wurlitzer organ (which still survives), on-stage fountains, leopard-skin seats and a 90-piece orchestra.

Such magnificence could not last for long. By the Sixties the variety shows and the swelling tones of the Wurlitzer were fast-fading memories. The Rank Organisation attempted to turn the Gaumont State into a rock venue. The Beatles, the Who and David Bowie trod its boards. Inside, thousands of teenage girls went berserk while out in the High Road thousands more, denied entry, created the kind of chaos which might have given even King Kong pause for thought.

Rank toyed with the idea of turning the Gaumont State into a shopping centre or amusement arcade. Shrinking from this solution, they retained most of the auditorium as a cinema and transformed part of the stalls into a ballroom and then a bingo hall.

In 1982 the Gaumont State, now considered the whitest of elephants, closed its doors. Three years later it was given a reprieve as a lavishly refurbished bingo hall, capable of keeping 1,500 pairs of eyes down for a full house. Today the principal reminders of the Gaumont State's glorious past are the black–and–gold pillars, the marble staircase and the chandelier which optimistically apes its big brother at Buckingham Palace. An amusement arcade and bingo now hold sway where once Clark Gable and Vivien Leigh melted into each other's arms in *Gone With the Wind* or Humphrey Bogart bade Ingrid Bergman goodbye at the end of *Casablanca*.

The Gaumont State is on the Kilburn High Road, NW6
Tube: Kilburn

HAM HOUSE GARDEN

In 1678 John Evelyn visited Ham House on the Thames near Richmond. He was greatly impressed by the beauty of the gardens, and wrote in his diary: 'After dinner I walked to Ham to see the House and Gardens of the Duke of Lauderdale, which is indeed inferior to few of the best Villas in Italy itself; the House is furnished like a great Prince's; the Parterres, Flower Gardens, Orangeries, Groves, Avenues, Courts, Statues, Perspectives, Fountains, Aviaries, and all this at the banks of the Sweetest River in the World, must needs be surprising'.

Were Evelyn to return to Ham House today, he would find the gardens virtually unchanged. Miraculously, they survived the 18th- and 19th-century fashion for natural landscaping. In 1975 work began on their restoration as part of the National Trust's contribution to European Architectural Heritage Year. They have been stocked with plants which flourished in English gardens of the 17th century, and surviving inventories show that most of them grew at Ham in its heyday, when the Duke of Lauderdale was a member of the Cabal, Charles II's inner Cabinet.

In those days gardeners were heavily influenced by the Dutch, whose tidy, managed countryside was mirrored in the formality of their gardens, with their geometrical shapes and neat, hedged enclosures. On the east side of the house is a charming parterre, known in the 17th century as the Cherry

Garden, where lavender and santolina grow in diamond lozenges edged with box and surrounded by yew hedges. Running down both sides are cool, shady arbours of hornbeam.

Below the terrace on the south front of the house, grass squares give way to the 'Wilderness'. This is a very ordered 17th-century version of the great outdoors in which grassy walks meander through a series of hedged enclosures dotted with small pavilions and, in summer, filled with wild flowers – ox-eye daisies, meadow saxefrage, bluebells and cowslips.

The work of restoration continues, and the next stage will see the embellishment of the Wilderness with statues and orange boxes. Head gardener Penny Hammond is also planning to transform the neighbouring rose garden into a 17th-century orna-mental kitchen garden, where blocks of vegetables and fruit trees, boxed by low hedges, will provide a feast of colour for the eyes and fresh produce for the refurbished restaurant in the Orangery.

The formality of the gardens at Ham can best be appreciated by viewing them from the upper floors of the house. As Penny Hammond observes, they instil a feeling of intense peace and well-being. They also retain the element of surprise which so delighted John Evelyn. Walking through the Wil-derness on a quiet weekday morning, one half expects a gentleman in court dress and periwig to drift out from behind one of Ham's tidily trimmed hornbeam hedges.

Ham House, Petersham, Surrey
Tube and Railway: Richmond, then 65 or 71 bus to
the Fox & Duck Inn, Petersham.
The house is open Tuesdays to Sundays inclusive, also
Easter Monday, Spring and August Bank Holidays 11
a.m. to 5 p.m. Admission charge. Children under 12
must be accompanied by an adult.

HANGING THE BUN
IN BOW

A strange little ceremony takes place every Good
Friday at the Widow's Son pub in Bow. A sailor

arrives to add a Hot Cross bun to the mouldering, shrunken and shrivelled collection of ancient and dessicated bakery hanging over the bar.

A sad tale lies behind this cheerful ritual. One Easter about 200 years ago a poor widow was waiting for her son's return from sea. To welcome him home she had baked a Hot Cross bun. But he never came; nor did any news of his fate. Every year thereafter she baked a bun in his memory, keeping the buns from past years as melancholy, if increasingly musty, tributes to his memory. In 1848 her humble home became a public house called The Widow's Son. Ever since, a Hot Cross Bun has been hung from the ceiling every Good Friday.

The Widow's Son pub is at 75 Devon Rd, Bow, E3 Tube: Bromley by Bow

HOUSE OF DETENTION, CLERKENWELL

Under the tarmac of a school play-ground in a quiet street near Clerkenwell Green lies a reminder of London's grim penal past, the subterranean remains of the House of Detention.

The first prison on the site was built in 1616. Jack Sheppard and his mistress Edgeworth Bess were imprisoned there in 1724 but escaped through the bars. Conditions were appalling and the prison

was described as 'a great brothel kept under the protection of the law for the emolument of its ministers'. It was rebuilt in 1773, and then put to the torch seven years later during the Gordon Riots. There were three more rebuildings, the last in 1844, which was modelled on the recently opened prison at Pentonville, then the last word in penal design.

Thereafter it was known as the House of Detention and became a holding prison for people awaiting trial. It was the busiest in London. Every year some 10,000 men and women passed through its gates, over which loomed a huge, gargoyle-like head whose matted hair, sunken eyes and screaming mouth symbolised criminal despair.

The meticulously kept records chronicle their

passage in poignantly cursory detail: 'John Driscoll, aged 15, possession of 6lbs lead. James Barret, aged 12, stealing a wine glass and other articles. Septimus Morgan, 25, attempting suicide'. Equally sad are some of the graffiti in the cells recorded in 1870 by the prison chaplain, the Reverend Horsley: 'All in a lonely cell I lie. No better I deserved. It will make your blood run cold to think how I got served'. Or, 'I was born in prison when my mother was doing a month for being drunk'. And 'For meeting a bloke in an alley and taking his ticker away'.

The authors of the *Criminal Prisons of London* encountered many affecting scenes when they visited the House of Detention: 'On visiting another cell . . . we found a fine-looking genteel boy, with beautiful English features. He had an oval face, blue eyes, rosy cheeks and curly hair. He was about twelve years of age, dressed in a dark faded overcoat and had been charged with stealing from a till. He was very poorly clad, and his shoes were in a wretched condition. He had been urged to steal by two young convicted thieves, who had made him their tool in the business while they had adroitly managed to escape. Soon after, his mother, a care-worn, poverty-stricken woman of about 35 years of age, came in, and was in extreme anguish when she saw her little boy. He burst into tears at the sight of his broken-hearted mother, but soon appeared to forget his own distress in her presence. The poor woman was convulsed with agony too deep for tears, and looked as if her heart would break. She pressed her hands to her throbbing temples, and seized hold of our arm to prevent herself from falling. She was led away to a seat outside the door of the cell, and was sitting there in silent anguish as we passed along the gallery'.

In 1867 two Fenian prisoners made an unsuccessful attempt to break out. A hole was blasted in the wall, demolishing a row of houses opposite and killing six people. The House of Detention itself was demolished in 1890. The perimeter wall survives as the school wall, and the Warder's cottage and the entire underground level of the prison were left intact. Some of the cells were used as air raid shelters during the Blitz. Other areas, including the so-called 'Dark Cells' where prisoners were punished, were sealed off and remain closed to this day. Now, for the first time in 100 years, the public can visit much of what remains. You enter along sinister ventilation corridors which lead visitors into the room where prisoners' clothing was fumigated, the kitchens and a cell block. A lively audio-visual presentation conveys some of the the site's melancholy history through the stories of individuals who passed through it. After the tour, fresh air and freedom come as something of a relief.

The House of Detention is in Clerkenwell Close, EC1
Tube: Farringdon.
It is open seven days a week from 10 a.m. to 6 p.m.
Admission charge. Tel: 0171 253 9494

JIMMY GARLICK: A MYSTERY SOLVED

High up in the ringing room of the west tower of St James Garlickhythe (an exceptionally beautiful Wren church on Garlick Hill in the City), is a heavy modern cabinet containing the dessicated corpse of a young man.

His head rests on a dark, tasselled cushion. Time has hunched his broad shoulders and made talons of his finely manicured hands. His upper lip is drawn back over a good set of teeth. It seems as if he is drawing a deep breath, hundreds of years long, before levering himself up to greet you.

He was discovered in 1855 during the clearing of the Vicar's vault. To generations of parishioners he has been affectionately known as Jimmy Garlick. Several medieval Lord Mayors are buried in St James, and some said he was Dick Whittington. Others claimed that he was a 17th-century thief who had hidden from his pursuers in the vestry and had suffocated there. For many years Jimmy was kept, upright, in a cupboard built specially for him in the church's inner vestibule. Naughty choirboys sometimes took him out and sat him in the choir stalls with a ruff around his neck. Everyone was fond of him, but nobody knew who he really was.

Recently, a possible solution to his identity was advanced by Julian Litten of the Victoria & Albert Museum. A clue is contained in a cartouche wall mounument at the west end of the church's north aisle: 'Here lieth interred the body of Seagrave Chamberlain. Eldest son to ye Honourable Colonell Edward Chamberlain of Northamptonfhire and fometime refident at Barbados. Which Seagrave departed this life December the 17 1675. Aged 16 years'.

Seagrave and Jimmy could be one and the same. The British Museum is of the opinion that the corpse is that of a late adolescent who died about 300 years ago. According to the church registers, Seagrave died of a fever while working as a servant (probably secretary) to a Mr George Butler. Seagrave's wealthy merchant family, sugar planters in Barbados, would have been influential enough to secure Seagrave's interment in the Vicar's vault at St James as an alternative to transporting his body back to Northamptonshire or the Caribbean. It is likely, but unproven, that Seagrave's employer was in the sugar trade.

Seagrave did not have a charmed life but in death he has become a great survivor. He is now awaiting a high-tech wash and brush up by the Victoria & Albert Museum before going back on public display. His handsome new casket – which cost more to make in 1993 than the rebuilding of the entire church after the Great Fire – displays a salutary message: 'Stop Stranger Stop As You Pass By. As You Are Now So Once Was I. As I Am Now So Shall You Be. So Pray Prepare to Follow Me'.

St James Garlickhythe is on Garlick Hill EC4
Tubes: St Paul's, Mansion House, Bank

JOE ORTON'S DEFACED BOOKS, ISLINGTON CENTRAL LIBRARY

A small, scurrilous slice of our literary heritage can be found in the Central Library in Islington, stamping ground of London's 'chattering classes'.

In May 1962 all the chattering was about Joe Orton and his lover and future killer Kenneth Halliwell. Long before Orton became a successful playwright, he and Halliwell hit the headlines when they were both sentenced to six months imprisonment for stealing 72 books from Islington's Central Library and wilfully damaging a number of others by removing their colour plates.

Orton and Halliwell had been smuggling books in and out of the library since 1959. Many of the plates from art books were used to decorate their bed-sit in Noel Road, the walls of which were covered from ceiling to floor with an extraordinary collage. Others were cut up and used to make intriguing modifications to the jackets and contents of pilfered library books. These were then replaced on the shelves, and the library itself became a small theatre as the couple surreptitiously observed borrowers' reactions to this handiwork on taking the books down.

Their efforts ranged from the surreal to the jokily

obscene. The jacket for John Osborne's *The World of Paul Slickey* sports a budgerigar. The abstract design on the cover of the *Collected Plays of Emlyn Williams* was enlivened with a number of typed messages including 'Olivia Prude', 'Knickers Must Fall' and 'Fucked by Monty'. Some of the juxtapositions are genuinely disturbing. On the jacket of a critical study of John Betjeman is a potbellied old man, tattooed from head to foot and wearing a pair of sagging swimming trunks. Orton's most successful paste-up was of Dame Sybil Thorndike locked up in a cell as Edith Cavell. A man peers through a window at her. What he sees is the stately Dame Sybil staring fixedly at the huge male genitalia of a superimposed Greek statue. A caption reads: 'During the Second World War I was working from dawn to dusk to serve the many thousands of sailors, soldiers and airmen. American GIs came in shoals to my surgery and some had very peculiar orders for me'.

The two would-be literary outlaws also stuck down new typed blurbs on the flyleaves of numerous books. One of the most celebrated turned a Dorothy L. Sayers whodunit into a sado-masochistic fantasy about a lesbian policewoman, WPC Brenda Coolidge, and a seven-inch dildo discovered in the 'Police Barracks'. It concludes, 'READ THIS BEHIND CLOSED DOORS! And have a good shit while you are reading!'.

The typing led to the couple's downfall. For 18 months Sidney Porrett, Islington's legal clerk and a character who might have stepped straight out of one of Orton's plays, had been hot on their trail. 'Plainclothes' librarians had cruised the shelves, noting their every move. A case was assembled against them, but one piece of the jigsaw was missing – a sample of their typewriting to see if it matched that on the books. Porrett sent them an official letter complaining about a car abandoned outside the bedsit in Noel Road. Halliwell rose to the bait, firing back an outraged reply, signing off 'Yours Contemptuously'.

The typefaces matched and the triumphant Porrett swung into action. Noel Road was raided by the police and the stolen material uncovered. After the trial at Old Street Magistrates Court, at which Orton was described by the defending counsel as a 'frustrated writer', the two miscreants were sent to separate open prisons. The 'frustrated writer' got his own back by pouring this experience into his savagely funny satires of mindless authority. Two years later he had his first stage success with *Entertaining Mr Sloane*.

The offending jackets and flyleaves are preserved at Islington Central Library, but are now too delicate to handle. However, the reference section will supply two books of colour photocopies on request. See for yourself what all the fuss was about and savour a strange relic of a literary apprenticeship and a doomed relationship.

Islington Central Library is in Fieldway Crescent, N5

Tube and Railway: Highbury and Islington.
Tel: 0171 609 3051

JOHN SNOW PUB,
SOHO

You can get an excellent pint in the John Snow pub
in Soho's Broadwick Street, but 140 years ago you
might have got something less agreeable – cholera,
the pestilence which stalked Victorian Britain for
much of the 19th century.

The opening-up of trade routes between Europe
and the East allowed cholera to spread from India
(where it was endemic) across the world. The
disease reached Britain in October 1831, and over
the next 30 years claimed hundreds of thousands
of lives. The symptoms were painless diarrhoea,
followed by vomiting and dehydration. 'King
Cholera' had a 50 per cent mortality rate, often
within hours and at the most within two days of its
onset.

No one knew how cholera was caused. Many
medical authorities believed it was spread by
poisoned air from putrefying bodies or rotting
vegetation. Among the bizarre suggested preventive
measures was the proposed use of cannon placed at
strategic points around London to 'disinfect' the
poisoned atmosphere. One man, though, had the
answer. He was Dr John Snow, Queen Victoria's

obstetrician, who in 1853 had administered chloroform during the birth of Prince Leopold. He believed that cholera was water-borne, a theory which was vindicated by his study of the 1854 cholera epidemic in Soho.

Snow's theory rested on his investigation of the public water pump in Broad Street (the present-day Broadwick Street), which was near his lodgings in Frith Street. He prepared a large-scale map of the area on which black lines indicated houses affected by cholera deaths. A casual glance at the map reveals a depressing concentration of deaths in the area around the pump, which the hapless locals prized for the purity of its water, and an almost complete absence of deaths around the other eleven pumps in the district. Snow wrote: 'There had been no particular outbreak or increase of cholera, in this part of London, except among the persons who were in the habit of drinking the water of the above-mentioned pump-well'.

Snow gave some striking examples. At a nearby brewery not one of the 70 men caught cholera because they were supplied with free beer or water from the brewery well. An army officer from St John's Wood dined in Wardour Street, drank the Broad Street water with his meal and was dead within hours.

Snow persuaded the authorities to remove the handle from the pump and the incidence of cholera rapidly fell away. His theory met with initial opposition, but his Soho findings, and similar research he conducted in Southwark and Vauxhall during the cholera outbreak of 1848–9, eventually led to radical improvements in London's sanitation and water supply. Snow did not live to see them, dying of a stroke in 1858 at the age of 44. In 1992 his pioneering work in scientific medical research was honoured by the erection of a pump – minus its handle – some 50 yards from the front door of the pleasant pub which bears his name.

The John Snow is on Broadwick Street, W1
Tube: Piccadilly Circus

KASPAR,
CAT EXTRAORDINAIRE

The oldest 'working' cat in London lives in the Savoy Hotel. His name is Kaspar, and he has reached the ripe old age of 68.

Kaspar's story begins in 1898. Just before leaving for South Africa, the diamond king Joel Woolf held a dinner party for fourteen at the Savoy. One guest cancelled at the last minute, but Woolf dismissed the superstition that whoever left the table first would die first. A few weeks later Woolf was dead, gunned down in his office in Johannesburg.

Fearful of precipitating a similar self-fulfilling prophecy, the Savoy subsequently arranged for parties of thirteen to be joined by a member of staff,

but this proved inconvenient if private matters were being discussed. Kaspar was the solution. In 1926 Basil Ionides was asked to design a three-foot-high black cat which he carved from a single piece of plane tree. Christened Kaspar, his home is in the Pinafore Room, one of the hotel's private dining rooms, where he perches elegantly on a high shelf in front of a large Art Deco mirror in which he can admire himself. Whenever a party of thirteen is lunching or dining at the Savoy, Kaspar is taken down to join them. He is seated in a fourteenth chair, with a napkin neatly tied around his neck, and is treated as a guest. A bowl of milk stands before him, sometimes supplemented by a bottle of whiskey, and his place settings are changed with each new course.

Kaspar is an extremely handsome cat, sleek and self-satisfied, with ears pinned back, sharp teeth bared and tail elegantly curved around his smooth haunches. In the Pinafore Room he keeps distinguished company. One of its panelled walls is lined with framed photographs of Prime Ministerial members of The Other Club, founded in 1911 by F.E. Smith and Winston Churchill. Over his shoulder Kaspar can exchange knowing looks with Ted Heath and Jim Callaghan. In the corner a large bust of Churchill waves a cheerful V-sign in Kaspar's direction.

Members of The Other Club, mostly politicians from both Houses of Parliament, dine regularly in the Pinafore Room. Churchill, who regarded Kaspar with great affection, always insisted on his attendance, and he has not missed a dinner with the Other Club since 1927. The story goes that Kaspar was once kidnapped by some roistering RAF officers and borne off to Singapore. On Churchill's orders he was immediately flown back.

Kaspar is a cat who could tell a tale or two but, like the Savoy, he remains the soul of discretion.

The Savoy Hotel is on the Strand, WC2
Tube: Charing Cross

KEW BRIDGE
STEAM MUSEUM

Rising serenely over Brentford is the slim Roman-esque tower of the old Kew Bridge pumping station, once the nerve centre of the Grand Junction Water-works Company and now the home of a unique steam museum housing the world's biggest collection of large steam engines.

The museum's pride and joy is the Grand Junction's 90-inch Cornish beam engine, named after the diameter of the huge cylinder inside which a BBC-TV camera crew recorded a party to celebrate the engine's return to work in 1976. Made in Cornwall in 1895, the 90-inch is now the biggest steam engine working anywhere in the world.

There are few more majestic sights in London than this magnificent engine in action. The rise and fall of the 35-ton beam is like a huge moving sculpture. Below the beam the huge cylinder plunges up and down, glistening with the water that runs down its sides. Steam arises from vents in the floor accompanied by the deep sucking and gurgling of the water being pumped below.

The sheer size of the engine, supported by dignified Doric columns, is testimony to the heroic scale of Victorian engineering. As the museum's general manager, Tony Cundick, observes, 'If they wanted more power, they just built it bigger'. And indeed, in an adjacent engine room stands an even bigger beam engine, the 100-inch built between

1869 and 1871. This black behemoth was maintained as a stand-by for many years after the other engines had been shut down in the early 1940s. It enjoyed occasional brief runs for the benefit of engineering societies, the last one being in 1958.

In their heyday the two engines ran day and night with an interconnection beneath the floor so that they made their strokes alternately. On the top floor of the engine house men oiled the bearings in and around the beams by the dim light of gas mantles, probably without stopping the engines. Below them, 14 men stoked the 14 boilers on three shifts. Add a driver for each engine, a greaser for both engines, a fitting shop, forge and office staff, and it is easy to see why these great engines cannot be used for commercial operations today.

Kew Bridge Steam Museum is on the corner of Green Dragon Lane and Kew Bridge Road, Brentford Tube: Gunnersbury (by District Line or North London Link). Railway: Kew Bridge. Admission charge. Tel: 0181 568 7432

KINGSBURY'S CASTLE

Suburbanites' homes have always been their castles, but in a leafy corner of Kingsbury in north London a real suburban castle rears up among the tidy ranks of half-timbered semi-detached houses.

Highfort Court, in Buck Lane, is a miniature version of the kind of fortress in which the Sheriff of Nottingham plotted his revenge on Robin Hood. Beneath its imposing tower, which conceals its chimney, a spectacular entrance worthy of the flamboyant Spanish architect, Gaudi carries the visitor over a basement 'moat' and under an arch guarding the block of flats which lies inside. The ramparts of the flat roof command sweeping views of Harrow on the Hill. Here residents can sunbathe or contemplate pouring boiling oil on the neighbours. On leaving, you notice two small bartisans (projecting turrets) with arrow-loop openings. They are not for directing a hail of fire on unwelcome visitors but for the more prosaic business of storing dustbins.

Highfort Court was designed by architect extraordinaire Ernest Trobridge (1884–1942). Between the wars, while many architects were experimenting with concrete frame, steel and glass, Trobridge was creating a suburban dream-world which drew on traditional English styles. In the 1920s, when building materials were scarce, Trobridge devised and patented a system of timber-framed house construction which combined an artfully contrived antique appearance with modern methods. In Kingsbury he used locally grown unseasoned elm for his houses, ensuring that adjustments could be made to floors and doors as the wood dried and shrank. Kingsbury is dotted with these delightful thatched houses, which seem more like the relics of a medieval village than the result of the speculative building in which Trobridge specialised. Inside, the houses are crammed with detail: stained glass, intricate brickwork, imposingly solid staircases and lots of curious nooks and crannies. Each house seems uniquely conceived, but all of them had a standardised framework which Trobridge calculated by using the width of a door as a module for the entire structure. All the windows were prefabricated.

In the 1930s, when building materials were plentiful, Trobridge turned to castles in brick and cement. His last project was a huge seaside hotel, the Ozonia on Canvey Island, which was intended to provide low-cost holiday accommodation for East-Enders. The Ozonia's interior was a riot of murals: a bedroom decorated as a monk's cell with demons squinting through cracks in the wall; a lounge transformed into an aquarium; and another populated by koala bears.

Trobridge was a devout follower of the Swedenborgian Church, subscribing to a philosophy which 'affects every detail of every structure, enabling one to divide each problem into end, cause and effect'. The dismal disciples of post-modernism could learn much from his inventive solutions to everyday housing problems.

Highfort Court is in Buck Lane, NW9
Tube: Kingsbury

LEIGHTON HOUSE

Behind the plain brick façade of the large Italianate villa at No. 12 Holland Park Road is one of the most remarkable interiors in London. Leighton House, the home of the artist and aesthete Frederic, Lord Leighton (1830–96), is the expression of one man's vision of a private palace devoted to art.

On entering the magnificently marbled and tiled hall, the visitor is greeted by a splendid stuffed peacock whose spectacular plumage is offset by the magnificent turquoise tiles designed for the hall and staircase by Leighton's friend William de Morgan. Turn left, past a life-size statue of a bearded and horned satyr, and you are confronted with the centre-piece of Leighton House, its Arab Hall.

The Arab Hall was created as a setting for the tiles Leighton had acquired on his travels in the Middle East. Designed by George Aitchison and based on the banqueting room in a Moorish palace in Sicily, the Hall conjures a Victorian dream of the Orient, a dazzling fantasy of the 1001 Nights. The artist Walter Crane was commissioned to design a frieze of fabulous animals around the walls. Hanging overhead is an ornate electrolier made of beaten copper and guilded wrought iron. In the centre of the Hall a fountain murmurs in the middle of a small pool, into which the artist Albert Moore once fell after a dinner party, disturbing two slumbering carp who thought it was time for supper.

Leighton's luxuriant fantasy extends throughout

the other rooms, not least in the upstairs studio which, in his day, was filled to overflowing with ornaments, tropical plants and artist's props. Here Leighton held his famous musical evenings, one of the hottest invitations in town, at which the great performers of the day played and sang. Empty now, the visitor must imagine the room banked with hothouse flowers, draped with tapestry and Oriental rugs and humming with a glittering throng of artists, literary types and aesthetes.

Here, surrounded by the rich, dense atmosphere generated by his collection of beautiful objects, Leighton lived a solitary life. The original plans for Leighton House, to which Aitchison later added the Arab Hall, included servants' quarters but only one bedroom and bathroom for the owner. Leighton did not want visitors to stay, as they interfered with his work.

The house is Leighton's autobiography in brick, stone and artefacts. In 1996, to mark the centenary of his death, Leighton's spirit will be evoked by recreating the house as it was during his lifetime. The public will be able to wander through the studio amid his paraphernalia of brushes, palettes and easels. And the dining room will be laid out for one of Leighton's formal bachelor parties at which visitors will be able to eavesdrop on the society and artistic gossip of late 19th-century London.

Leighton House is at 12 Holland Park Road, W14 Tube: High Street Kensington.

Curious London

It is open to the public (admission free) Monday to Saturday 11 a.m. to 5.30 p.m. Closed Sundays and Bank Holidays, For further information about guided tours, concerts, lectures and private functions, Tel: 0171 602 3316

LINLEY SAMBOURNE HOUSE, KENSINGTON

Behind the door of No. 18 Stafford Street, near Kensington High Street, lies a house locked in a Victorian time warp. Built in 1873, it was the home of the *Punch* cartoonist and photographer Edward Linley Sambourne from the year of his marriage to Marion Herapath in 1874 to his death in 1910. Today it remains almost exactly as it was in the 1890s, when Sir John Tenniel, Lewis Carroll's illustrator, came to dine off caviar and roast lamb and Oscar Wilde spilt a bottle of claret over Marion's dress.

No. 18 was an artistic home which reflected the taste of the Aesthetic movement of the 1870s: William Morris wallpaper, rich rugs glowing in the subdued light, banks of ornaments and bric-à-brac, and bright explosions of stained glass. In the dining-room at the front of the house, two stained glass roundels of Titania and Ariel filter the northern light dimmed already by blinds and lace curtains.

Everywhere, the walls are crowded with Linley

Sambourne's original artwork, massive in scale and featuring a bewhiskered cast of long-forgotten Victorian heroes and villains locked in national and international crises. They jostle for space alongside work by Walter Crane and Kate Greenaway, and an eclectic jumble of prints and drawings ranging from classical statuary to a grim-faced Napoleon retreating from Moscow. At the head of the first flight of stairs, light pours on to a ferny indoor water-garden housed in a projecting bay window. The splashing of its small fountain sends ripples of noise through the quiet of the house.

Linley Sambourne was an obsessive photographer. He could not draw without reference, and accumulated about 35,000 'cyanotypes', which are still being catalogued. He developed them in a deep coffin-shaped tank which can be seen in the bathroom on the half-landing between the second and third floors. On one of its walls hang several dozen cyanotypes of Linley Sambourne, bearded and benign, posing for the camera – in the attitude of Mr Punch, dressed as a cavalier, or encased in a suit of armour and brandishing a sword. Beside him, his groom, Ostler, is smirking and clad in the costume of a Roman emperor.

On another wall are the *risqué* photographs of servant girls, some of them painfully thin, which Linley Sambourne took for the Camera Club. His callous remarks about them in the diary he kept suggest a side which was less benign than the image conveyed by his jolly self-portraits, although they accurately reflect the views of both his time and class.

Linley Sambourne's camera occupies pride of place in the house's L-shaped drawing room. He also possessed a right-angled 'detective' camera, disguised as a pair of binoculars, which (rather creepily) he used to take sneak photographs of schoolgirls in the streets of Kensington. His favourites were given nicknames, a foible which, in those pre-Freudian times, did not apparently disturb his wife and fellow-diarist Marion.

Linley Sambourne's son, Roy, lived in No. 18 until his death in 1946. He never married and never changed a thing in the house. His bedroom reeks of Edwardian bachelorhood: Conan Doyle and Kipling on the bookshelves; signed photographs of pretty young actresses on the walls and the plush valanced mantelpiece; and Roy breezily posing with a bevy of chaperoned girlfriends in his Oxford days. The stained glass window in the bedroom depicts owls for night and swallows for morning. It throws a rosy glow on his father's original illustrations for The Water Babies.

In the 1960s No. 18 became the home of Anne, Countess of Rosse, Linley Sambourne's granddaughter and a founder of the Victorian Society, which now runs the house. Thanks to Lady Rosse, who died in 1992, the house transports the visitor effortlessly back to 1892, when hansom cabs rattled past the front door and the hall was rich with the smell of Linley Sambourne's Havana cigars.

The Linley Sambourne House is at No. 18 Stafford Terrace, W8
Tube: High Street Kensington.
It is open (from 1 March to 31 October) on Wednesdays from 10 a.m. to 4 p.m and on Sundays from 2 p.m. to 5 p.m. Groups at other times by prior arrangement. Tel: 0171 994 1019.

THE LONDON HYDRAULIC
POWER COMPANY

In the heyday of hydraulic power there were nearly 200 miles of water mains under the capital, operated by the London Hydraulic Power Company.

Millions of gallons of water, pumped by five stations through the mains at a pressure of 400 pounds per square inch, was used to operate lifts, hydraulic presses and wagon hoists, and to raise and lower cranes and West End theatre safety curtains. So powerful was the force of the water in the pipes that a safety official of the company had to be present at every public procession in the centre of London as a precaution against a bursting main, which could blow a huge hole in the road.

The London Hydraulic Power Company went

into decline in the 1940s. The development of
electric power, bomb damage in the Blitz when
many mains were broken, and the demolition of the
Edwardian mansions which were serviced by
hydraulic lifts, doomed the company to extinction
and it ceased to operate in the 1970s. Its dried-up
cast iron pipes now provide a home for coaxial
television cables – subterranean estate remains valu-
able property. The London Hydraulic Company
lives on in the manholes, marked 'LHP' set in the
pavement in front of the buildings it used to serve.

LONG WOLF'S RETURN

Until recently, one of the more colourful inmates of
Brompton Cemetery, in Earls Court, was a Red
Indian chief and warrior of the Oglala Sioux tribe,
Long Wolf.

He was buried there in 1892, having died of
pneumonia at West London Hospital while appear-
ing with Buffalo Bill's Wild West, a travelling
spectacular assembled by Colonel 'Buffalo Bill'
Cody which re-enacted the conquest of the West
with a cast of hundreds of real-life cowboys, Indians,
buffalo, elk, horses and cattle. In Cody's words the
tour would demonstrate to Europeans that 'the vast
region of the United States was finally and effec-
tively settled by the English-speaking race'.

Long Wolf was no ordinary native American. He

grew up in the Black Hills of Dakota, which his tribe believed was the centre of the earth. And it was in the defence of these hills – which contained large deposits of gold – that a war was fought against the US Cavalry by the Sioux, or Lakota as they prefer to be called ('Sioux', which means 'snake', was an insulting name bestowed on them by the French.) In 1876, at the Battle of the Little Big Horn, the Lakota and their allies, under Crazy Horse, defeated and killed the reckless and incompetent General George Armstrong Custer. Long Wolf who was a sub-chief to Crazy Horse, almost certainly fought in the battle, possibly as a scout. There is no doubt that he was a warrior: his autopsy, conducted by the appropriately named Dr Coffin of West London, pronounced him 'covered in gunshot wounds and sabre cuts'.

Re-enacting the defeat of his people for Buffalo Bill was a less dignified occupation for Long Wolf, even though the show attracted huge crowds. During Queen Victoria's Golden Jubilee celebrations of 1887 the Wild West played to houses of up to 40,000 at Earls Court, and Long Wolf would have been introduced to Gladstone and the Prince of Wales. Even the reclusive Queen Victoria came, venturing out for the first time as a widow. She later wrote: 'The cow boys (*sic*) were fine looking people but the painted Indians with their feathers and wild dress (very little of it) were rather alarming looking and they have cruel faces'.

Before he left for Europe, Long Wolf had a

premonition that he would die and expressed a desire that a wolf be carved on his tomb. He got his wish and then faded into history. It was only by a series of chances that his descendants in America discovered the whereabouts of his grave. There is a reference to Long Wolf's death in a book written by Robert Cunningham Graham, Scottish nobleman, adventurer and friend of Buffalo Bill. In 1991 a tattered copy of the book came into the possession of Elizabeth Knight, a Worcestershire housewife with a passion for Lakota history. It was Knight who managed to contact Long Wolf's descendants in the United States. In turn they obtained permission from the Home Office and Buffalo Bill's family, who owned the plot, to return Long Wolf's remains to the Black Hills.

But there was one more mystery to be solved. Buried above Long Wolf was another body, that of a Lakota child called Star Ghost Dog, who had also died on the tour. The Ghost Dog family was tracked down, and the remains of the little girl accompanied Long Wolf home, wrapped in buffalo hide. They were buried just a few miles from Wounded Knee, where in December 1890 the US cavalry killed 150 Indians in a massacre which has become a symbol of white aggression towards the original inhabitants of America.

Long Wolf has now gone home but other distinguished residents in Brompton cemetery include Francis Fowke (the architect of the Albert Hall), the writer George Borrow, Sir Henry Cole (the organising genius of the Great Exhibition and the Victoria & Albert Museum), and the suffragette Emmeline Pankhurst.

Brompton Cemetery is on the Old Brompton Road, SW10
Tube: West Brompton.

LONDON'S SMALLEST HOUSE

The smallest house in London, at 10 Hyde Park Place, is owned by the nuns of the Tyburn convent. It is only 3ft 6in wide. The bottom storey is an alleyway behind the front door and the upstairs room served as a bathroom.

Theories abound about the origins of the house. It might have been a watchman's gate looking out on to the old St George's graveyard at the rear, where body snatchers flitted in and out of the shadows. It was from this graveyard that, in 1768, the freshly buried writer Laurence Sterne was smartly removed by grave robbers and rushed round to a surgeon for dissection. The surgeon, a literary man, recognised the recently deceased author of *Tristam Shandy* as he was slapped down on the slab and promptly had him re-interred, an incident which could have sprung straight from the pages of Sterne's picaresque masterpiece.

More prosaic reasons for the erection of this tiny

dwelling might have been to block off a public right of way or a need to establish a London residential qualification. After inspecting 10 Hyde Park Place, you might consider proceeding to an interesting companion piece, the phantom houses of Leinster Gardens in Bayswater. These are Nos. 22 and 23, which seem perfectly normal in that elegant street. But stop and look more closely: the windows are empty black voids; the doors will never open. The houses are nothing more than a façade, blocking the view of the Metropolitan Railway running below. This was the price extracted by local residents when two five-storey houses were knocked down in the 1860s to let through London's, and the world's, first underground railway. From the back, Nos. 22 and 23 look like a film set.

10 Hyde Park Place, W2
Tube: Marble Arch. Nos. 22, 23 Leinster Gardens,
W2. Tube: Queensway, Lancaster Gate.

THE LOOS OF
OLD LONDON TOWN

Apart from being provincial boys who made good in the big city, what do Dick Whittington and Joe Orton have in common? As Lord Mayor of London in the early 15th century, Whittington built one of the city's first public lavatories, a 24-seat unisex affair by the side of the Thames, grandly known as 'Whittington's Night Soil House of Easement'. Over 500 years later, Joe Orton was wont to take his ease in public lavatories, cheerfully 'cottaging' his way across the London of the 1950s.

Even after Whittington's thoughtful intervention, there was scant provision for people caught short in medieval London. Malodorous shacks clung to the edge of the City's ditches and streams, often clogging the water-courses beneath them with ordure. These latrines were regularly cleaned out by gangs of 'gongfermers', who were well paid for their dirty and sometime's dangerous work. At least one of them, known as 'Roger the Raker', fell into a midden and drowned.

Such amenities as flush toilets, developed at the end of the 16th century, were only for the rich and powerful. Elizabeth I installed one at Richmond Palace, but most people relied on chamber pots.

A familiar sight in the streets was the 'human lavatory', equipped with bucket and voluminous cloak, behind which his paying customers squatted, concealed from the prying eyes of passers-by. Many Londoners were less modest. You only need change one letter in Clerkenwell's Passing Alley to divine its original use. The tiles in Prudent Passage near Cheapside proved so tempting to people in need of relief that local householders erected gates at each end. They were torn down by the mob.

Victorian sewage systems, and the invention of the 'S-trap', ushered in the Golden Age of the public lavatory. Visitors to the Great Exhibition in Hyde Park in 1851 were provided with quaintly named 'monkey closets' designed by George Jennings. Over the next 40 years magnificently appointed conveniences – tiled, brass-railed and gleaming with mahogany – appeared across London. Handsome wrought ironwork, pergolas and lamp brackets advertised their presence and persuaded the public to 'spend a penny', the price of admission. One of the most magnificent, in High Holborn, boasted a cherub beaming down at customers from the foul air pipe and, from the 1920s, goldfish swimming happily in its glass cisterns. The original fittings were dismantled in the early 1980s and are stored in the Museum of London. As the Victorian era drew to a close, the public convenience became a symbol of municipal pride, although some wags pointed out that it had taken London 1,500 years to catch up with the Romans.

In 1937 the social historian Thomas Burke wrote a learned book on London's loos. One of his conclusions was that their location and availability was bound up with the British class system: 'Places are most frequent in those districts where there is large consumption of tea and beer; least frequent in those districts where sherry and claret rule'. Using this principle, Burke pointed out that South London was well served by public conveniences, but the posher purlieus of Mayfair, South Kensington and St John's Wood were virtually no-go areas for those with straining bowel or bladder.

Sadly, many of the finest Victorian loos have been buried under tons of concrete or boarded up. The latter fate has overtaken the charming iron pissoir in Star Yard, near Fleet Street, with its royal crests and three marble urinals. Others have been converted. The substantial lavatories built in Arts and Crafts style at the bottom of the Lillie Road, in Fulham, have been turned into offices. Next door stands a reminder of their former function – one of the modern Tardis-like unisex monstrosities which differ from Dr Who's Time Machine only in the fact that they are considerably *smaller* on the inside than their exterior would suggest. On Shepherds Bush Common the loos built for the benefit of crowds on their way to the 1908 Olympics at White City have been turned into a snooker club.

One exception to the dreary functionalism of modern loos can be found in Westbourne Grove, near the Portobello Road. Thanks to the efforts of local residents, and the imaginative work of architect Piers Gough, a striking new loo has risen on the site of its in-filled Victorian predecessor.

The slim, triangular, tiled building, with its fan-like roof, is reminiscent of the Art Nouveau look of the Paris Metro. There's a nautical feel to it, too. Its sea-green tiles and elegant low brick prow suggest a submarine surfacing from the deep, water cascading down its sides. Bobbing behind, like a rowing boat in tow, is a Victorian drinking fountain. The prow is bright with plants from the flower shop built around the front of the loo, and a pleasing

round clock juts jauntily out at one side. At the
entrance life-size dancing male and female figures
beckon you in. In 1994 Piers Gough's loo won a
Royal Fine Arts Commission architectural award.
An entire new category, that of *jeu d'esprit*, was
created to accommodate it. It's worth a detour to
have a look.

A different range of figures welcomes you to the
upstairs toilet of the eclectically decorated Sun pub
in Clapham Old Town. If you want to take your
ease in a fair approximation of a rain forest, albeit
one situated in south-west London, then the Sun is
the place for you.

Here we have Nature, green in tooth and claw.
The toilet-goer in the Sun will never be more than
a couple of feet away from some of the more slithery
members of the rainforest's fauna, among them
snakes, spiders, bats and a lizard. A cascading
waterfall, just waiting for the arrival of Tarzan and
Jane, covers the wall behind the mosaic-tiled cistern,
and, to complete the effect, a tape-recording of
jungle noises is activated to alarm unwary visitors
the moment they open the door. A smoky mountain
rises on one of the loo's blue-green walls and an
exotic bird covers the inside of the door. Parrots
and butterflies dance before the dazed eyes of heavy
drinkers, while the profile of a jungle tribesman,
hopefully not a head-hunter, ensures that the occupant will never feel alone.

This remarkable interior was designed by Royal
Academy-trained Caroline Ward. At first she was

unsure about how to tackle the project: 'I started off with the waterfall and toyed with the idea of having fish everywhere, but the forest seemed to grow by itself. On the whole people seem to be very enthusiastic about it'.

The nearest Tube stations to Piers Gough's loo are Notting Hill Gate and Ladbroke Grove. The Sun pub is a stone's throw from Clapham Common Tube station.

NATHAN'S THE TOBACCONIST

A rich, if politically incorrect, aroma spills out from Nathan's at the bottom of Richmond Hill. Run by the amiable Nat Chait, this charming little shop is a shrine to smoking in all its forms.

The window is packed with smokers' impedimenta and ephemera, 'the associated pieces', as Nat calls them – tobacco tins, pipe smoker's knives and pipe reamers. In advertisements for dimly remembered brands of tobacco, tweedy, firm-jawed types straight from the pages of John Buchan puff contentedly at pipes stuffed with quality tobacco because they are 'the people who know'.

Framed cigarette cards celebrate the skills of baggy-shorted, brilliantined footballers of long ago. Or remind passers-by of the half-forgotten profiles of a clutch of minor movie stars. Trapped in their frames, nut-brown county cricketers of the 1930s dream of halcyon pre-war summers.

Inside, Nathan's is a small cave of delights. Behind the battered Edwardian counter a huge mirror extols the virtues of Abdullah cigarettes, their trademark a stern-looking sepoy surrounded by a laurel of palm leaves. On the counter a tall, gleaming brass lighter swivels neatly to light your Burma cheroot.

The white walls are lined with music-hall posters, among them the doughty male impersonator Hetty King topping the bill at the Chiswick Empire ('Private Boxes 10/6d') and a colourful array of the display material which has decorated traditional tobacconists' premises since Victorian times. In the smoker's heyday – the long Edwardian summer – there were hundreds of brands from which to choose. Where have they all gone: Ardarth Straight Cut, Sea Horse Cork Tipped and Clarke's Dusky Maiden?

In those days the shadows had not closed in on the smoker. Every packet of the turn-of-the-century Pick Me Up Straight Virginias carried the stamp 'For the Benefit of Mankind'. An old advertisement for Kensitas – a brand still on sale in Scotland – proclaims 'Just What the Doctor Ordered' as a solemn butler proffers a packet on a silver salver. On another a Thurberesque little man in a hospital bed refuses the nurse's thermometer with the immortal words, 'No thanks, I'd rather have a Kensitas'. A sub-text there for ASH, surely.

Nat Chait's range is more limited these days, but he still has snuff for sale. Many years ago, when he started out in the trade, snuff sales were kept buoyant in the mining regions. Miners often took a box of snuff down the pit since they were not allowed to smoke underground. But there are few miners now, and a diminishing population of smokers. Tucked away in a corner of Nat's shop is a wonderfully dotty sixties' attempt to make snuff trendy – a display card in which a bouffant-hair-styled, 'dolly bird' secretary takes a snort of snuff (well, I assume it's snuff) before pounding out a memo on her Olivetti.

Nat has been in the business for 50 years and his shop evokes a vanished world when smoking was not frowned upon. His collection of smoking ephemera has provided the launching-pad for a society dedicated to the art of the cigarette packet which now has 200 members worldwide. Nat needs little prompting to burst into rhapsodies about the artwork of a pre-1914 packet of Virginia Beauties sold by Singleton and Cole of Birmingham. Keen collectors pay big money for these little masterpieces.

Those who have forsaken the demon weed might find the longing for a puff creeping back if they pop their heads round Nat's door, but his shop is well worth a visit, even if only to swap a few yarns with its ever-welcoming proprietor.

*Nathan's is at the bottom of Hill Rise, Richmond,
Surrey*
Tube and Railway: Richmond

OLD ENGLISH SKITTLES
AT THE FREEMASONS ARMS

It's Thursday night at the Freemason's Arms on
Downshire Hill in Hampstead, and something is
stirring in the basement. As Sherlock Holmes used
to bark at Dr Watson, the game's afoot. But the
game in question is no subterranean devilry hatched
by Professor Moriarty. The Hampstead Lawn, Billiards & Skittles Club is playing a National Westminster Bank team at Old English Skittles.

Celebrated by Pepys and Dickens, and played
enthusiastically by A.P. Herbert, Old English Skittles, or London Skittles as it's often called, was once
the most popular game played in pubs above the
Pool of London, particularly those which lay along
the river. As late as the early 1950s, it was played in
dozens of pubs. Now only three venues remain: the
National Westminster Sports Club at Norbury, the
Duke of Devonshire in Balham and the Freemasons,
where until 1972 you could also play the ancient
game of pell mell, a cross between golf and croquet
enjoyed by King Charles II.

Old English Skittles is a more robust game than
the 'long alley' version played in the West Country.

In the basement at the Freemasons, nine pins, made of hornbeam oak and looking like First World War shells, stand on a diamond-shaped frame also made of hornbeam. The skittler stands 21 feet away, swinging a heavy wooden discus, called a 'cheese', which is lobbed underarm at the pins. At the end of the court a plaque warns the players to maintain 'Silence on the Stroke'.

The teams of six players compete head to head in a game which lasts until closing time. Considerable skill is required to maintain accuracy with the cheese, which is made of the tropical hardwood *lignum vitae* and weighs up to 12 pounds. The game has a rich vocabulary of technical terms, among them 'Cocked Hat', 'London Bridge' and 'the Gates of Hell', the last describing a fiendishly difficult shot, as hard to pull off as a golfing hole in one.

In the midst of all this unabandoned throwing, scoring and drinking, two unfortunates are consigned to the 'pit'. It is their job to put up all the fallen pins or 'deads' once a player has completed his frame. This task is known as 'sticking', and like 'chalking' at darts has to be performed in order to be next on the play list. The stickers also adjudicate over disputed shots and 'fallers', pins which drop without being struck and are not counted.

The survival of London Skittles hangs by a thread. Replacing the elderly cheeses is a problem as the importing of *lignum* is now banned. The equally aged hornbeam pins also take a terrible battering from the ponderous projectiles thrown at them. But the enthusiasm of the skittlers ranging from octogenarians to young men in their twenties, is infectious. The only current woman player, artist and tour guide Jamie Jamieson-Black, attempted to get the game going in Russia on a recent visit. The Old English Skittlers of Putney, the 'Aquatics', are keen to restore the disused alley in the basement of the Dukes Head, near Putney Bridge. At the moment they have to play away in Balham.

Guy Tunnicliffe, the club secretary at the Freemasons, likens the small skittling community to the 'last mating pair of dodos', but interest in the game is growing, and it may not be too long before more riverside pubs reverberate with the rattle of cheese on hornbeam pin.

The Freemasons is on Downshire Hill, NW3
Tube: Hampstead. Railway: Hampstead Heath

OLD OPERATING THEATRE
AND MUSEUM, ST THOMAS'

One of the most intriguing and macabre historic interiors in London is to be found in the garret of St Thomas' Church, Southwark, on the original site of Thomas' Hospital. It is the oldest surviving operating theatre in the country.

The garret above the church was already being

used by the hospital's apothecary to prepare medicinal herbs when, in 1822, part of it was converted
into a purpose-built operating theatre for women.
The female surgical ward was next to the garret.
Distressingly for the patients, operations took place
on the ward. Additionally, the theatre's location let
in the natural light needed to speed the surgeon's
knife in the days before anaesthetics and antiseptic
surgery.

The theatre was closed and bricked up in 1862
when the hospital moved to Lambeth. It lay forgotten, preserved by its seclusion in the roof space of
the church (which became Southwark Cathedral's
chapter-house) until it was uncovered in the 1950s
and restored. Now it is the centre-piece of a
remarkable medical museum.

Under the skylights, on stubby legs and looking
like a butcher's block, stands the wooden operating
table. Rising around it are the standings from which

Old Operating Theatre

medical students, 'packed like herrings', watched the surgeons. Speed was of the essence. An amputation would take a minute or less, and operations were timed with the same breathless attention as Grand Prix cars making a pit stop. Cheers rang out at the end of a particularly speedy piece of knife-work.

Little or no attention was given to hygiene. Surgeons operated wearing old frock coats stiff with congealed blood and pus, and often they washed up only *after* they had finished. Their instruments were laid out on a cloth-covered table crawling with bacteria. Below the operating table, which was covered by an oilcloth over a blanket, stood a square box filled with sawdust which the surgeons deftly kicked this way and that as they worked to catch the blood running from their patients. Beneath the theatre's floorboards was a false floor, creating a space which was packed with more sawdust to ensure that any blood which escaped the box did not drip on the worshippers below. It also served as effective sound-proofing.

The hair-stuffed chairs around the operating table were for the use of distinguished visitors. All the personnel in the theatre were men. The surgeons were attended by 'dressers', their senior male apprentices, and female nurses were barred from the theatre. Stifling in summer and freezing in winter, the operating theatre was a house of pain, but one in which the basis of the medical vocation

Curious London

was not forgotten. High on the wall a sign in Latin
reads, 'Compassion, not Gain'.

The Old Operating Theatre is at 9a St Thomas
Street, E1.
Tube and Railway: London Bridge.
It is open from 10 a.m. to 4 p.m., Tuesday to Sunday.
Admission charge. Tel: 0171 955 4791/0181 806 4325

PEACE PAGODA, BATTERSEA PARK

In the late-summer heat joggers puff past the
London Peace Pagoda in Battersea Park. From its
northern niche a golden image of the Buddha gazes
serenely across the Thames to the Chelsea
embankment.

The Pagoda, which was completed in May 1985,
was a gift of the the Most Venerable Nichidatsu
Fujii and the Japanese Buddhist order he founded,
Nipponzan Myohoji. It is one of 70 such Pagodas,
all of them dedicated to peace, which the order has
built worldwide. There is another one in Milton
Keynes. Based on ancient Japanese and Indian
tradition, the Pagoda is over 100-foot high with
walls clad in slabs of reconstituted Portland Stone.
Its elegant canopies are made of 500–year-old yellow
Douglas fir. Around the central tower, in niches,

are four large gilded statues of the Buddha set against coloured backdrops. At night the Pagoda is floodlit by low-intensity lights set around the base platform. The slim green bronze pinnacle at the top of the Pagoda carries seven umbrellas and is topped by a gilded kota, a kind of spiritual weathervane ringed by eight golden wind bells. Similar wind bells hang from the corners of the canopies.

The Pagoda, which radiates a feeling of order and calm, can be seen as a map of spiritual life. The base represents the earth and stable energy, the white central domed tower the flowing energy of water. The upward energy of fire is represented by the roofs, and the saucer dish at the base of the umbrella-shaped crown symbolises air and free energy. The kota at the top represents consciousness and eternal spirit. Sacred reliefs of the Buddha are enshrined inside the fabric of the Pagoda.

Since its completion, the Pagoda has been a focus for peace activities. Two hundred yards away, screened by trees, is a small temple associated with the Pagoda. The monk-in-residence, the Reverend S. Nagase, beaming and resplendent in his saffron robe, greets visitors with a sonorous chant and an offering from the Buddha, in my case a toffee from a large bowl of sweets.

Behind the monk rises a bank of golden Buddhas. Below them are small clumps of offerings – including Marmite, a carriage clock and a packet of cornflakes – an odd contrast to the temple's beautiful and brightly coloured Tibetan prayer flags. At my request the Reverend Nagase squatted to strike the temple's magnificent ceremonial drum, whose rib-rattling tones reverberate around the small room. The dense, sun-splashed foliage pressing against the windows hides Battersea Park from view and, as the drumbeats die away, temporarily transports the visitor to a world of Eastern mysticism. Outside a new wave of sweat-soaked joggers plough past the Peace Pagoda.

To become a Friend of the Peace Pagoda, contact the Park Manager's Office, Battersea Park, Albert Bridge Road, London SW11 4NJ Tel: 0171 228 2978

PET CEMETERY,
HYDE PARK

Tucked away behind the railings at Victoria Gate, on the Bayswater Road, is one of the more unusual burial sites in London – a cemetery for cats and dogs.

In a shady plot behind the classical gate house lies a little pet necropolis. It's a graveyard in miniature, crammed with the tiny marble tokens of affection raised for pets long dead by owners who have long since followed them to the grave. The cemetery grew up in the early 1880s around the grave of 'Cherry', a Maltese terrier that belonged to a Mr and Mrs J. Lewis Barnes. When Cherry was

followed by the Duchess of Cambridge's dog, a fashionable precedent was established. By 1893, 33 little tombstones had risen on the site. In 1967 the last (and approximately 300th animal) was buried there – 'Prince', a Marine Commando dog whose substantial gravestone reads, 'He Asked for So Little and Gave So Much'.

The inscriptions bear witness to the affection in which these privileged animals were held. One suspects that the majority were the pampered pugs, pekes and poodles owned by the fashionable women of Bayswater: 'Our Dear Little Curio', 'Darling Tsing', 'Sweet Baby Quita' and a small pack of 'Spots'. A raffish note is struck by 'Jack the Dandy, a Sportsman and Gentleman', doubtless a bustling Jack Russell terrier.

We know the history of some of the dogs buried

at Victoria Gate. 'Topper', for example, was the mongrel mascot of the King Street police station at Westminster. According to an article in the *Strand* magazine of 1893, 'Topper' was a dog of 'thoroughly dissipated habits' who ate himself to death. He was put out of his misery in appropriate fashion, with the business end of one of the constabulary's truncheons.

In this overgrown haven dogs and cats are united in death. One grandiloquent gravestone commemorates 'Ginger Blyth of Westbourne Terrace – A King of Pussies'. Turn-of-the-century London knew nothing of political correctness, as is attested by the large number of black cats named 'Nigger' buried here. Interred in tasteful cloth bags, their bones have fertilised this small secret garden that provides an enduring reminder of the incorrigibly sentimental attitude of the English towards their pets. It was all too much for George Orwell, who in his essay *The English People*, described this feline and canine Boot Hill as 'perhaps the most horrible spectacle in Britain'.

London's sole Nazi memorial is a tombstone to a dog called Giro, with its German epitaph honouring 'A true friend!'. It can be found in Carlton House Terrace alongside the steps leading up to the Duke of York column and close to what was Nazi Germany's London embassy. Giro belonged to Leopold von Hoesch, the ambassador who was succeeded by the champagne salesman and subsequent Nuremberg defendant Joachim von Ribbentrop.

The little terrier met his end in 1934 when he tarried a little too long in the vicinity of an exposed electric wire.

The pet cemetery is not a public place but permission for a visit can be obtained from the Royal Parks Agency. Tel: 0171 298 2000

POSTMAN'S PARK

Postman's Park is a charming green oasis near St Paul's cathedral, so-called because of its proximity to the General Post Office in King Edward Street. On summer days postal workers can be seen taking their lunch-breaks here, feeding crumbs to the pigeons.

The park was opened in 1880 and comprises the churchyard of St Leonard's Foster Lane, St Botolph's Aldgate and the graveyard of Christ Church Newgate Street. More land bordering Little Britain was added in 1883. It's a soothing, sheltered place, where the only discordant note is struck by Michael Ayrton's ferocious statue of the Minotaur, horned, hung like a prize bull and ready to trample over the prim flowerbeds which ring his plinth.

If the Minotaur took off in a headlong charge, he would probably bring down a small lean-to construction in his path. Its sloping roof protects one of the most melancholy memorials in London. In

1887 the sculptor and painter George Frederick Watts dreamed up the idea of a national monument to humble folk who had lost their lives while trying to save others. In 1900 the idea became reality, and a wall in Postman's Park was dedicated to plaques singing a sad litany of people who perished while trying to rescue drowning companions or workmates trapped by fires and explosions. Typical of their deeds is the story of 'Daniel Pemberton, aged 61, foreman LSWR, surprised by a train when gauging the line, hurled his mate out of the track, saving his life at the cost of his own, Jan 17 1903'.

There are numerous plaques here, in elegant ceramics, each with a clipped but telling tale to tell. 'Sarah Smith, Pantomime Artist at Prince's Theatre, died of terrible injuries received while attempting in her inflammable dress to extinguish the flames which had engulfed her companion, 24 Jan 1863.' And 'Godfrey Maule Nicholson, manager of a Stratford distillery, and George Elliott and Robert Underhill, workmen, who successively went down a well to rescue comrades and were poisoned by gas, 12 July 1901'. Ponder these poignant plaques while munching a lunchtime snack.

Postman's Park is off King Edward Street, EC1
Tube: St Paul's

POST OFFICE RAILWAY

The Post Office solved the problem of moving mail quickly around London by going underground. Work on its underground railway started in 1913 but was interrupted by the First World War. The tunnels ware completed in 1926 and the railway was opened in 1927. Within a year one quarter of London's mail vans disappeared from the streets.

The six-mile-long railway, which runs from Whitechapel to Paddington, is powered by electricity and fully automatic. The 27-foot-long trains have four containers which can carry 15 bags of letters or six bags of parcels. Up to 50,000 bags of mail are carried each day. The stations on the line are connected by a series of shafts to the sorting offices above. Designed to avoid accidents, each section of track goes 'dead' after the driverless train passes over it. During peak periods there is a train each way every four minutes travelling at speeds of up to 35 m.p.h.

PRINCE HENRY'S ROOM,
FLEET STREET

In the bustle of Fleet Street, it's easy to miss the sign for Prince Henry's Room. Those who follow it up a narrow flight of stairs can savour a small slice of London's 17th-century past.

Prince Henry's Room, at No. 17 Fleet Street, is on the first floor of one of the few houses in the City to survive the Great Fire of London in 1666. The history of the site can be traced back to the 12th century when it formed part of the property held by the Knights Templar, but the present building dates from 1610 when an inn called The Prince's Arms was built there.

The Prince in question was Prince Henry, son of James I and elder brother of the future Charles I, who in 1610 became the first Prince of Wales in 100 years. On the ceiling of the room named after him, his accession to the title is reflected in the superb enriched Jacobean plastering which bears his three feathers and the letters 'P' and 'H' in a star-shaped border.

At the age of 18 Prince Henry was carried away by a fever. He was a keen swimmer and his death may well have been caused by a water-borne infection. There is no evidence to suggest that Prince Henry had any personal connection with the room, although the story persists that it was used as the Duchy of Cornwall's council chamber.

Between 1795 and 1816 the front part of the house was occupied by a waxworks museum run by a Mrs Salmon. She put a false front on the building and replaced much of the fine oak panelling in Prince Henry's Room with chocolate-coloured pine. Fortunately, her vandalism did not extend to the west wall, where vistitors can still examine the small wooden dowels which are all that holds the original panelling together.

In 1900 the London County Council purchased and restored the building. Its false front was removed to reveal the 17th-century half-timbered front, shorn of its bay windows by Mrs Salmon but with the essential features intact and almost entirely preserved under thick layers of paint. In Prince Henry's Room the plasterwork was hidden under 17 layers of paint and grime. The handsome stained-glass windows were installed a few years later.

Prince Henry's Room also contains an exhibition of 'Pepysiana' originally assembled by the Trustees of Pepys House at Brampton, Huntingdon, and purchased by the Corporation of London in 1985. The great diarist was born near Prince Henry's Room in Salisbury Court, Fleet Street, on 23 February 1633 and in later life may well have enjoyed a glass or two at the Prince's Arms, which from 1665 was known as The Fountain. A charming guide with a truly Pepysian name, Thomas Good-fellow, provides the public with a lively history of the room and a racy summary of Pepys' eventful life.

Prince Henry's Room is at No. 17 Fleet Street, EC4.
The room is open Monday to Saturday from 11 a.m.
to 2 p.m.
Tube: Chancery Lane. Tel: 0181 294 1158

PUTNEY HEATH OBELISK

Hidden away in the woods of Putney Heath, close to the Kingston Road, is a monument to a bizarre experiment in which George III, not yet mad but distinctly peculiar, was an unwitting participant.

In March 1774 the King and his wife Charlotte took breakfast at Putney with David Hartley MP, doughty opponent of the slave trade, friend of Benjamin Franklin and scientific investigator. Hartley was the inventor of a system of fireproofing, intended for houses and His Majesty's Ships, which he chose to test in a most unusual way.

While the royal couple sipped their coffee in a first-floor salon, Hartley's servants set fire to the room below. The King and Queen finished their meal unaware of the conflagration raging beneath them, protected by the copper and iron plates which Hartley had installed under the floorboards.

Hartley's experiment earned him the Freedom of the City and a gift of two and a half thousand pounds. His house has long since gone and all that marks the spot where he played with fire is the obelisk. In spite of his spectacular approach to market testing, Hartley was a dull old stick, described as being 'destitute of any personal recommendation of manner' but nevertheless 'possessed of some talent with unsullied probity added to indefatigable perseverance and labour'. In Parliament his speeches were so intolerably long and tedious that 'his rising always operated like a dinner bell'.

The Putney Heath Obelisk can be found on Putney Heath near the Telegraph public house, Telegraph Road.
Tube: East Putney. Railway: Putney.

SIR JOHN SOANE'S MUSEUM, LINCOLN'S INN FIELDS

London is dotted with 'Gothick' fantasies and follies, the legacy of the Romantic movement that was all the rage among the chattering classes in the early years of the 19th century. One of the most remarkable examples is to be found in Sir John Soane's Museum at No. 13 Lincoln's Inn Fields.

Sir John Soane (1753–1837) was the architect of the Bank of England and a supreme collector at a time when the English upper classes were busily buying European art treasures by the ton. Soane's home of many years, two adjoining terraced houses in Lincoln's Inn Fields, is not only a monument to his acquisitive tastes but also his highly developed sense of humour.

In the bowels of the building is the 'Monk's Parlour', an elaborate joke which Soane made at the expense of all those who (like him) subscribed to the fashionable cult of antiquarianism. The Parlour's occupant was the imaginary 'Padre Giovanni', whose 'tomb' and ruined 'cloister' can be seen in the courtyard outside. The cloister was built of miscellaneous medieval fragments, most of which Soane had salvaged from the old Palace of Westminster. They are surmounted by a Corinthian column, on the top of which teeters a bust of the Duke of York, an architectural conceit which would amuse today's post-modernists. The Padre's classical tomb contains the remains of Lady Soane's dog and bears the legend 'Alas, Poor Fanny'. Inside the Parlour, casts of dozens of medieval gargoyles leer down at a skull on a table in the centre of the room. At the back, the monk's cell contains an even more impressive *memento mori* – a complete skeleton.

Sadly, the joke turned sour. Soane's wife died in 1815, and in later years the distraught architect spent much of his time brooding in the contrived gloom of Padre Giovanni's parlour.

The Monk's Parlour is only one part of an extraordinary house that contains a magnificent Venetian scene by Canaletto and *The Election* and *The Rake's Progress* by Hogarth. The panels in the Picture Room housing the Hogarths swing back to reveal the Monk's Parlour below. The Room was cunningly designed to accommodate enough pictures to fill a gallery more than three times its length. Not only are the pictures hung right up to the ceiling but the north, south and west walls consist of hinged planes inside which more pictures are stored. Architecture was Soane's dominating

Sir John Soane's Museum

Curious London

interest, and the Picture Room contains magnificent architectural drawings by Piranesi and Clerisseau. The planes also contain a watercolour by Turner. On the south side of the room, the planes open to reveal 12 large drawings of Soane's work, including an imaginary view of the Picture Room.

Classical statuary, architectural models and drawings and pre-Columbian pottery (which Soane considered most 'uncommon') fill every nook and cranny of the museum space he created at the back of the building. The prize exhibit is the sarcophagus of the Pharaoh Seti I, which Soane purchased in 1824 for £2,000 when the British Museum baulked at the price. Soane displayed the sarcophagus 'by lamplight', creating a sensation in London society.

In the oldest part of the museum, known as the Dome, is a marble bust of Soane, presented to him in 1830 by his friend, the sculptor Sir Francis Chantrey. When Chantrey finished the bust, he wrote: 'Whether the bust ... shall be considered like John Soane or Julius Caesar is a point that cannot be determined by either you or me. I will, however, maintain that as a work of art I have never produced a better'. There can be few if any houses in London so full of original effects of light and space and so crammed with curiosities of all kinds: Wren's wrist-watch, pistols belonging to Napoleon and Peter the Great, a scold bridle for nagging wives, shackles for slaves, a German cross-bow, a 'flint stone in the shape of a human foot' and a huge fungus from Sumatra. Soane stipulated that the house should remain unchanged after his death, and this wish has been honoured. Visitors can move through his unique creation much as he did over 150 years ago.

In the spring of 1995 the Soane Museum opened two rooms unseen by the public for many years.

These are Soane's breakfast parlour, which has been meticulously restored to its original state and is linked by double doors to a new gallery designed to show a selection of the 30,000 architectural drawings which Soane collected. A series of elegant glass and steel cabinets, the work of Eva Jiricna, are the first sign of 20th-century design in the museum, and their arrival sparked off a lively architectural row, which Soane would have probably have relished.

Sir John Soane's Museum is at 13 Lincoln Inn Fields, WC2
Tube: Holborn.
The museum is free and open from Tuesday to Saturday, 10 a.m. to 5 p.m. Also on the first Tuesday evening of each month from 6 to 9 p.m. Tel: 0171 405 2107. Information Line 0171 430 0175

ST BRIDE'S
FLEET STREET

When, in December 1940, Luftwaffe bombs tore the heart out of the beautiful Wren church of St Bride's in Fleet Street, they revealed layer upon layer of London's hidden history.

An archaeologist, Professor W.F. Grimes, was brought in to excavate the church's crypt, which for centuries had been used as a burial chamber and charnel house. Conditions for its inmates were crowded: in 1664 Samuel Pepys had to bribe the grave-digger with sixpence to 'jostle together' bodies to make room for his recently deceased brother Tom.

Grimes' work showed that the church, which Wren built five years after its predecessor had been destroyed in the Great Fire of London, stood on a site that had been in continuous occupation since Roman times. There were some fascinating finds, from the skeleton of a Roman woman given a Christian burial to the crushed coffin of the 18th-century novelist Samuel Richardson. Lying below the church were the levels of London laid down by time, stretching from the Romans through a 6th-century Irish settlement and Saxon and Norman periods to the perpendicular chuch built in the 15th century by William Vyner, warden of the Fleet prison, whose name was punningly celebrated in stained-glass depictions of grapes and vines.

The long association of St Bride's with the printed word began when a printing press was brought to Fleet Street by Caxton's assistant, the appropriately named Wynkyn de Worde, who was buried in the church in 1535. Fleet Street may now have been dispersed all over London, but the connection is maintained. St Bride's was the focus for the campaign waged by the Friends of John McCarthy.

The church positively hums with history. Its magnificent spire, topped with a ball and vane, inspired an 18th-century pastry cook, William Rich, to model his wedding cakes on this 'madrigal in stone'. The

St Bride's

cakes were laced with lots of brandy, at 'one guinea a bottle'. One of the dresses worn by Rich's wife is on display in the crypt's museum which is funded by the newspaper industry. At the early morning service in the crypt, worshippers can gaze past the altar to the remains of a Roman mosaic pavement. Among the items on display is a gruesome patent iron coffin from the early 19th century, designed to thwart grave robbers in search of bodies for dissection.

On Easter Sunday the congregation spills out of the church to roll coloured hard-boiled eggs down Fleet Street. The egg which travels the farthest from St Bride's wins a modest prize.

St Bride's Church is on Fleet Street, EC4
Tube: Chancery Lane

ST PANCRAS: THE MIDLAND GRAND HOTEL

St Pancras was a 14–year-old Christian boy who was martyred in Rome in AD 304 by the Emperor Diocletian. In England he is rather better known as a railway station. And not just any railway station. St Pancras, terminus of the Midlands Railway, the most solidly Victorian of railway lines, is one of the great Victorian buildings of London. It inspired a rhapsodic description from John Betjeman, who wrote of the 'cluster of towers and pinnacles seen from Pentonville Hill and outlined against a foggy sunset and the great arc of Barlow's train shed gaping to devour incoming engines, and the sudden burst of the exuberant Gothic of the hotel seen from gloomy Judd Street'.

In March 1995 one of the glories of Victorian London, the former Midland Grand Hotel at St Pancras, was opened to the public for the first time in 60 years. The visitors who thronged through its doors were not able to book a room or buy a meal. Indeed, the Midland Grand was not looking at its best. The wallpaper was peeling, the residual plumbing was antediluvian and the temperature inside was Arctic. Nevertheless, they were in for a treat, crossing the newly scrubbed floor mosaics in the entrance hall to drink in an atmosphere still rich with the expansive confidence of the high summer of Empire.

The station was completed in 1868, and in that year work began on the hotel, designed by the most eminent architect of the time, Sir George Gilbert Scott, a firm believer in the Gothic as the only 'Christian' architectural style. The hotel was opened to the public in 1873, and at the time it was by some way the most magnificent in London. It was one of the first to have lifts, which were called 'ascending rooms' and worked by hydraulic power (see London Hydraulic Power Company, p. 97). In 1890 the hotel opened the first ladies's smoking room in London.

The hotel's design of pinnacles, towers and gables bore more than a passing resemblance to Scott's rejected plans for government offices in Whitehall. In his memoirs, Scott wrote of the hotel: 'It is often spoken of to me as the finest building in London; my own belief is that it is possibly too good for its purpose, but having been disappointed through Lord Palmerston of my ardent hope of carrying out my style in the Government Offices . . . I was glad to be able to erect one building in that style in London'.

By 1935, when the Midland Grand closed its doors, Scott's ornate style was derided by modernist architects. The great building was chopped up and partitioned into offices which eventually became the headquarters of British Rail's Traveller's Fare. The spectacular interior became as insipid as a plastic cup of British Rail tea. Drab public-sector paint coated the elegant walls; intricate plasterwork languished behind artificial ceilings. By the 1960s, when Betjeman wrote about it, the principal remaining feature of the hotel was the Grand Staircase which 'ascends the whole height of the building by an unbelievably rich cast iron series of treads with stone vaulting and painted walls. The chief suites of rooms are on the first floor and the higher the building, the less important the rooms, until the quarters for the servants are reached in the gabled attics – men on one side and women on the other – and separate staircases. Yet even these are large and wide and compare favourably with more modern accommodation'.

By then St Pancras had been targeted for demolition and was saved only after a vigorous campaign led by the Poet Laureate. Betjeman was convinced that architectural tastes would change, and it is sad that he has not lived to see the final proof of his prediction. Fittingly, a new railway era has come to the rescue of St Pancras, which is now seen as a splendid 'gateway to Europe' – if and when the station becomes London's Chunnel terminal for the 21st century.

The exterior of the building has been given a ten-million pound face-lift. An interior survey undertaken by the specialist architects Margaret and Richard Davies has confirmed that many of the original features have remained relatively intact beneath layers of magnolia and battleship grey. Paint has been stripped away to reveal majestic marble, green Connemara and Red Devonshire limestone, gilt, stencilled patterns and sumptuous wallpaper. The extravagant medievalism of the foyer, with its mosaics and marbled pillars, makes it a meeting place worthy of King Arthur and the Knights of the Round Table. The stone vaulting at the top of the Grand Staircase celebrates a cathedral of Victorian capitalism.

The cost of restoring the Midland Grand as an hotel and conference centre is estimated at about £50 million, a small price to pay, perhaps, to remind us of a time before we became Little England.

The open days initiated by British Rail in March 1995 were temporarily curtailed while work was put in hand to ensure that the parts open to the public conformed with fire regulations. For further information about access to the Midland Grand Hotel ring 0171 607 9909

SOME STATUES
AND AN EMPTY SPACE

William Makepeace Thackeray in conversation with the Brontë sisters; Queen Boudicca sallying forth against the Romans; the first man to be killed in a railway accident. All are part of London's rich collection of statues.

Thackeray's conversation piece can be seen in Cornhill in the form of a deep relief carved in mahogany by Walter Gilbert in 1939. Boudicca and her daughters bring a slightly disorderly martial spirit to the Victoria Embankment. How they would have managed in battle, careering around in a chariot without reins, is something of a puzzle. Passers-by will look in vain for any resemblance between the avenging warrior queen and the Duchess of York, who in a famous 1994 spoof news story was offered the role of Boudicca in a putative film by maverick director Ken Russell.

The model for the statue of Edith Cavell in St Martin's Place could have been a real movie star – Anna Neagle at her most heroically refined. Cavell gazes towards Trafalgar Square radiating polite

reproach to the Germans who shot her as a suspected spy in 1915. Under Cavell's feet are her
slightly ambiguous words, 'Patriotism is Not
Enough'. Behind her rears an ugly granite background, one of whose inscriptions, 'Faithful unto
Death', makes her seem more like an aged Labrador
retriever than a war heroine. When the monument
was unveiled in 1920, a General murmured to
Margot Asquith, 'The Germans will blush when
they see this'. To which Margot is said to have
replied, 'Won't the British?'.

The toga-clad Victorian gentleman in Pimlico
Gardens is William Huskisson, first victim of the
Railway Age. Huskisson, a former president of the
Board of Trade and a notorious ditherer, was mown
down by Stephenson's Rocket during the opening
of the Liverpool-to-Manchester railway on 15 September 1839. The Rocket ran over his leg at the
thigh and, according to a witness, 'crushed the limb
to a jelly'. Huskisson died in agony several hours
later. His anguished cry of 'It's all over with me;
bring me my wife and let me die!', ushered in an
new age of mass transport.

Poor old Huskisson died as he had lived: in Paris
in 1789 he was nearly trampled to death by an
enraged mob on its way to storm the Bastille; on his
honeymoon he fell off a horse and broke his leg.
And his statue, somewhat inappropriately garbed
given the circumstances of his death, had an equally
chequered career. It was originally presented to
Lloyd's Insurance Hall but was removed after the

clerks there complained that Huskisson had never been a member. It arrived in its present position, courtesy of the London County Council, in 1915. Osbert Sitwell, in his *People's Album of London Statues*, wrote the wretched Huskisson off as an 'unparalleled nonentity' and described the statue as 'boredom rising from a bath'.

The writer Desmond McCarthy always maintained that the best-dressed statue in London was the bronze monument to Viscount Palmerston (Prime Minister from 1855 to his death in 1865), which stands in Parliament Square. He wrote, 'The frock coat fits like a glove, and though the trousers do not break on the instep, to suit modern taste, the hang of them is magnificent'. McCarthy considered that the statue should be an 'object of pilgrimage to all the tailors of England'. Less conventionally clothed statues in London include the founder of the Scout movement Lord Baden-Powell in Queen's Gate, complete with shorts, woggle and knobbly knees; Alcock and Brown, the first men to fly the Atlantic, looking splendid in their aviator's gear at Heathrow Airport; and Captain Robert Falcon Scott, the doomed explorer, striking out in full Arctic kit in Waterloo Place.

The politest statue in London is Prince Albert, raising his hat in Holborn Circus. The most prudently attired is Sir Sidney Waterlow in the park which bears his name in Highgate; he is equipped with an umbrella. In the church of St Andrew's Undershaft, Leadenhall Street, the bust of John

Stow, the great 16th-century chronicler of London, is furnished with an even more practical accessory, a real quill pen in his hand. Every year the Lord Mayor or his representative gives Stow a new pen as a tribute to the abiding value of his *Survey of London*, published in 1598 and the first book to record the city's streets, buildings and events. The *Survey* was both history and a guide-book. Stow wrote, 'What London hath been of ancient time men may here see, as what is now every man doth behold'.

An interesting royal statue is that of William III on horseback in St James's Square. The monument shows the molehill which tripped his horse and killed him. After the fatal accident the King's enemies would drink a toast to the health of 'the little gentleman in velvet'. A more than usually royal statue is the rather stiff likeness of Queen Victoria in front of Kensington Palace in Kensington Gardens. Dated 1893, it is the work of her daughter Princess Louise. It was in Kensington Palace that the 18-year-old Victoria was woken at 6 a.m. on one cold June morning to be told of her accession to the throne by Lord Conyngham and the Archbishop of Canterbury.

London has only one surviving figure of Queen Elizabeth I surviving from her own lifetime. Dated from 1566, it can be seen in a niche on the wall of St Dunstan's in the West, Fleet Street. The statue originally stood over the Ludgate entrance to the City. It survived the Great Fire of London unscathed.

Next to Palmerston in Parliament Square is the South African soldier and statesman Jan Christiaan Smuts. He strides purposefully forward, his hands clasped behind his back, Duke of Edinburgh style, but there seems something very odd about his head. It is disproportionately large because the sculptor, Jacob Epstein, was misled about the height of Smuts' plinth. The heads of statues are usually oversize so that they appear normal when viewed from below. Epstein overcompensated, and was furious when the statue was unveiled.

Trafalgar Square is crowded with statues, although when asked few people can come up with more than Admiral Nelson, keeping lonely station on top of the column designed by William Railton. Looking down Whitehall is an equestrian statue of Charles I. Flanking Nelson's column are two Victorian military worthies, Generals Havelock and Napier, the latter once described as 'the ugliest statue in London'. Tucked underneath the balustrade on the northern edge of the square are the busts of three naval men: Admirals Jellicoe and Beatty, heroes or villains of the Battle of Jutland in 1916, depending on your view of naval history; and the most recent addition to the square's furniture, Admiral Cunningham, victor of Cape Matapan in 1940 and later First Sea Lord. Cunningham's bust appeared in 1966, three years after his death.

Controversy dogged the busts honouring Jellicoe and Beatty. The two admirals heartily loathed each other in life, and in death Jellicoe's widow strenuously objected to her husband sharing a public place with an 'officer of lesser rank'. By the time the row had subsided, the Second World War had arrived to delay the busts' appearance by several more years.

Outside the National Gallery pedestrians hurry past a stern George Washington and James II, sculpted by Grinling Gibbons and looking rather camp in Roman military gear. They are dwarfed, however, by a huge equestrian statue standing on a pedestal in the north-east corner of the square. A slimline version of the roué monarch George IV sits astride a handsome steed and gazes with an optimistic eye in the direction of Drummond's Bank. With neither saddle nor stirrups he would doubtless have experienced the same problems of control as Boudicca.

There should be at least one more statue in the square. In the north-west corner, a corresponding pedestal to the one occupied by 'Prinny' has remained untenanted, except for pigeons, since Sir Charles Barry laid out the square in the 1840s, though in the summer of 1995 the Fine Arts Commission invited suggestions for a new occupant. It had been originally planned to fill the pedestals with statues of George IV and William IV, but the money ran out. The statue of George IV which now stands in the square had been privately commissioned by its subject and remained homeless until it was placed on the north-east pedestal as a temporary measure which somehow became permanent. At one point it was threatened with removal to Virginia Water, 'preferably to the bottom of the lake', as one wag observed, but it has gamely clung to its perch.

Trafalgar Square has always been something of a moveable feast as far as its statues have been concerned. Long before it was laid out, the statue of Charles I had a lively history. It was made in 1635 by the Huguenot Hubert Le Sueur and closely modelled on the statue of Henri IV by the Pont Neuf in Paris. It was originally destined for a site in Roehampton, but eventually ended up in the churchyard of St Paul's church in Covent Garden. When the Civil War broke out it was consigned to the crypt in St Paul's, but was later seized by Parliamentarians in 1655. The statue was then sold to a Holborn brazier, one John Rivet, to be melted down for its brass. Rivet, however, was a canny operator. He hid the statue and went on to market all manner of items, from spoons to candlesticks, which he claimed were from the melted-down statue. Triumphant Roundheads brought them as souvenirs of the late unpleasantness as readily as did inconsolable Cavaliers.

With the Restoration the statue re-emerged and was installed in its present position in 1677. On this site in October 1660 eight of the men who had signed Charles I's execution warrant had been half-hung and then cut down and disembowelled. Samuel Pepys recorded the death of one of them, observing that he looked 'as cheerful as any man could in that condition . . . his head and heart were shown to the people, at which there was a great shout of joy'. Charles' satisfaction at occupying this sanguinary location must be tempered by the fact that only a few hundred yards away in Whitehall he lost his own head. A bust marks the spot.

Controversy and financial problems swirled around the erection of Nelson's column like a London pea-souper of old. Landseer's lions took 25 years to make their appearance at the base of the column, and in the process their seemingly interminable gestation became one of London's longest-running jokes. There was a statue of General Gordon in the square until 1943 when it was removed to make way for a Lancaster bomber in 'Wings for Victory' week. The unfortunate Gordon never made it back to 'London's front room' and was eventually relegated to a site on the Embankment.

STONE OF LONDON, CANNON STREET

If you bend down to peer through a smeared window set in the wall of the Overseas Chinese Banking Corporation at 111 Cannon Street, you will see a small rounded stone. An unspectacular sight, perhaps, but this is the fabled 'Stone of London'.

The origins of the stone, a weathered Clipsham limestone, are, as they say, uncertain. It was certainly present in the Cannon Street area as far back

as 1198, when it was referred to as the Lonestone. When Jack Cade, led the men of Kent in rebellion to London in 1450, he struck the stone with his sword and declared, 'Now is Mortimer Lord of the City!'. (Mortimer was the name he had assumed for this enterprise, hoping to identify with the family of King Henry VI's rival, the exiled Richard, Duke of York.) The stone did not prove much of a talisman for Cade. He had the satisfaction of executing the hated Lord Treasurer, James Fiennes, but within three days Londoners had tired of mob rule and sent Cade and his rebels packing. Their leader was wounded and captured near Lewes and died at Heathfield while being transported back to London.

In Tudor times it was believed that the stone was a Roman milestone, possibly the one from which all measurements in the province of Britannia had been taken. Later theories suggested that it was the

Street Scenes

rounded top of an early wayside Roman funerary
monument.

In 1742 the stone was removed and set in the
wall of St Swithin's, an outstandingly beautiful
Wren church which was destroyed by German
bombs in 1941. Thereafter it found a home with the
Bank of China, quite near the honoured spot it
occupied during the Middle Ages.

A clue to the origins of the Stone of London
came from the excavation, in the 1960s, of a palatial
Roman building under Cannon Street railway
station. Its mosaic pavements, large ornamental pool
and spectacular garden terrace looking out over the
the Thames suggest that this was the official residence of the Roman Governor. Perhaps the Stone
of London formed some part of this building and,
in consequence, had a special significance for the
city's medieval inhabitants.

Tube: Cannon Street

STREET SCENES

London's streets are packed with curious details and
embellishments. Behind many of them lie stories
which throw a sideways light on the life and history
of the city and its people. All the observant pedes-
trian needs to do is look up and around.

On the wall of the Shakespeare's Head pub in

Curious London

Carnaby Street, high above shoppers' heads, is a lifelike bust of William Shakespeare gazing quizzically down at the throng below. Carnaby Street is now little more than a tatty tourist-trap relic of the days when it was at the hub of Swinging London. Shakespeare might be about to intone the line he gave King Lear: 'I do not like the fashion of your garments; you will say they are Persian attire, but let them be changed'.

A tablet on the wall of the George Inn, Wanstead High Street, tells the tale of two builders who on 17 July 1752 were working on some scaffolding. A pieman passed below with a tray of tempting pies on his head. The lads bent down and relieved him of one of them. They were caught in the act and fined half a guinea. They subsequently carved an inscription recording their heinous crime, 'in Memory of ye Cherry pie', which reads, 'As cost half a Guiney ye 17 of July. That day we had good cheer. Hope to do so many a year'.

The cow's head on the wall of a house in Old Church Street, Chelsea, marks the site of a vanished dairy. Cows were kept in the back of this building until 1914. Dairymen used to buy cows which had recently calved and then kept them in backyards, and even basements, for a few months until their milk ran dry. The cows were then returned to the farms and exchanged for new milkers. Below the cow's head in Chelsea is a beaming sun, added when the premises became an antiques business.

Mice are commemorated on a 19th-century

building at the corner of Eastcheap and Philpot Lane in the City. While the masons were at work on the carvings that decorate the building they became the victims of a plague of mice. An affectionate little carving, above a scallop bearing the name of the building's architect, shows two of the little fellows tucking in to some of the masons cheese. They might have attracted the attention of one of London's best-known felines, Dick Whittington's cat, who is immortalised in stone on Highgate Hill in north London. Although his cat is a familiar, albeit fictional, figure in pantomime, Whittington was real enough, serving as Lord Mayor of London on three occasions, in 1398, 1407 and 1420. The

legend that the cat played a part in Whittington's
success probably stems from the story that he made
his fortune from coal. Medieval coal barges were
known as 'cats'. At the spot on Highgate Hill where
his cat is commemorated, Whittington – then
young, poor and leaving London – is supposed to
have heard the Bow Bells telling him to 'turn again'.

All that remains to remind us of the St James'
Theatre which once graced King Street (off Piccadilly), are the heads of Laurence Olivier and Vivian
Leigh as Antony and Cleopatra, forming part of a
frieze on the anonymous office building which rose
on the site in 1959. The theatre had seen some great
names in its day. In the 1890s Oscar Wilde's plays
opened here, and the playwright and his Salome are
commemorated above Larry and Viv. The dynamic
duo managed the theatre from 1950 to 1954, scoring
a big hit in a double bill of *Caesar and Cleopatra* and
Antony and Cleopatra. Later, Terence Rattigan's
Separate Tables ran at the St James' for two years,
but not even this could save the theatre from the
attentions of the new breed of property developers
who, in the late 1950s, were turning swathes of
London into an architectural wasteland. When the
freeholders of the St James' sold out in 1957, Vivien
Leigh launched a national campaign to save the
theatre. There was a debate in the House of Lords,
which the temperamental star interrupted from the
public gallery before being gently led away by Black
Rod. Winston Churchill coughed up £500 for the
fighting fund, but at least £½ million was needed

and was not forthcoming. The men in suits scored another dismal victory over a much-loved London landmark.

Look up at the clock on the church of St Dunstan in the West in Fleet Street and you will be greeted by a most unusual sight. It was erected in 1671 by parishioners to give thanks for the church's escape from the Great Fire. It consists of a bracket clock which originally projected over the street and an Ionic temple containing two loin-clothed figures wielding heavy clubs with which they half-heartedly strike a bell every 15 minutes. The figures are, in all probability, those of the legendary giants Gog and Magog, Ancient Britons who fought the Trojans thousands of years ago. Statues of Gog and Magog, who are medieval clones of a single giant called Gogmagog, were a prominent feature of 15th-century pageants and processions. In 1554 they greeted Queen Mary on her entry into London, and four years later did the same for Queen Elizabeth. There are two large limewood statues of Gog and Magog in the West gallery of the Guildhall.

The clock which the giants enliven in Fleet Street is said to be the first London clock to have minutes marked on the dial, and the first with a double face. It's something of a literary timepiece. References to it can be found in Goldsmith's *The Vicar of Wakefield*, Dickens' *Barnaby Rudge* and Cowper's *Table Talk*, where it is described thus: 'When Labour and when Dullness, club in hand/Like the two figures of St Dunstan's stand/beating alternately in measured time/The clock tintinabulum of time'. In the 1830s, when the church was rebuilt, the clock was bought and removed by the Marquess of Hertford who re-erected it in his villa, in Regent's Park, a desecration which brought tears to the essayist Charles Lamb's eyes. It was restored to its rightful place by newspaper magnate Lord Rothermere in 1935.

At the church of St George the Martyr, in Borough High Street, the church clock has four faces, three of them white and illuminated at night and one of them black and unlit. The white faces look towards the Borough district whose residents contributed towards a church appeal. The black face is turned reproachfully towards the parish of Bermondsey, whose tightfisted parishioners declined to give charitably.

London's oldest street advertisement can be seen on the wall at 63 King's Cross Road. It lacks the impact of the Wonderbra campaign of 1995 but more than makes up for it with its discreetly ancient charm. A bearded face looms above the legend, 'This is Bagnigge House Neare the Pindar a Wakefielde 1680'. The Pindar was a local tavern, and there is still a pub of that name nearby. Bagnigge House, owned by a local family, the Bagnigges, was said to have been the summer retreat of Nell Gwynne, who entertained Charles II there with concerts, breakfast and (no doubt) much more besides. In the 18th century it became a popular spa and pleasure gardens where, according to the

London Magazine of June 1759, 'Ye gouty old souls and rheumaticks crawl on,/here taste the blest springs, and your tortures are gone . . .'.

The slabs of stone outside the Athenaeum Club, at 107 Pall Mall, look rather like an elongated Olympic medal winners' podium. They were placed there at the request of the Duke of Wellington so that he could mount his horse more easily. At the southern end of Piccadilly, near Hyde Park Corner, is an odd shoulder-high shelf on two slender pillars. It's a porter's rest erected in 1861 by the vestry of St George's Church, Hanover Square, 'for the benefit of porters and others carrying burdens'.

Many of the bollards on London's pavements are made from ships' cannons discarded after various 18th- and 19th- century campaigns and surmounted by cannon balls. This recycling process was reversed during the Second World War when in August 1940 a scheme was launched with the initial aim of collecting half a million tons of scrap – enough, so it was said, to build 300 destroyers. Down came the railings from London's streets and squares amid accusations of 'sabotage' and 'vandalism'. By September 1944 the total weight of railings demolished had reached one million tons, many of which got no farther than the huge rusting piles on to which they were dumped.

London is littered with relics of the Second World War, most of them unnoticed. At the western end of Putney Bridge Tube station, for example, there is a large brick pill-box. Now daubed with graffiti, it is one of the thousands built in 1940 when invasion threatened. It commands an excellent field of fire over the surrounding streets below, but its exposed position would have made it very vulnerable in any last ditch battle for London. During the Blitz thousands of Londoners sought refuge from the bombs in their Anderson shelter, a corrugated-iron construction sunk in the back garden which, it was said, could withstand anything but a direct hit. In an allotment in North Sheen, and in many others throughout the suburbs, rusting Anderson shelters now serve as tool-sheds. The anonymous metal railings outside the council flats on Dog Kennel Hill, East Dulwich, are in fact stretchers which were once used to carry air raid victims. Similar railings can be seen in Church Street, Camberwell. Another half-hidden reminder of Britain's finest hour, and of the class divisions in British society, can be seen in the directions to air raid shelters which remain in two very different streets. On the wall of a town-house in Westminster's Lord North Street, residents are politely informed of 'Public Shelters in Vaults under Pavements in This Street'. In Deptford High Street, in contrast, a surviving sign consists of a large 'S' accompanied by an arrow and '60 yds'.

A little known fact about Trafalgar Square is that at each corner are the lamps from Nelson's flagship HMS *Victory*. Originally oil lamps, they were converted first to gas and then to electricity. Lamplighters were given a bonus for cleaning them as they are so large. Also on display in Trafalgar Square are the imperial standards of length, from one inch to 100 feet, which were set up under the square's north parapet in 1876.

Not far from Trafalgar Square, in Horse Guards Parade, is one of the more spectacular items in London's gallery of street furniture. The Cadiz cannon is a huge squat artillery piece mounted on a cast-iron Chinese dragon on which an inscription reads: 'To commemorate the raising of the siege of Cadiz in consequence of the glorious victory gained by the Duke of Wellington over the French near Salamanca, 22 July 1812. This mortar cast for the destruction of the great fort, with powers surpassing all others, and abandoned by the besiegers during their retreat, was presented as a token of respect and gratitude by the Spanish nation to HRH Prince Regent'.

Slightly less respect was attached to the cannon's subsequent history. It was christened the Regent's Bomb (which in those days was pronounced 'bum') and it became a favourite subject for caricaturists. The Cadiz cannon was depicted in saucy terms in numerous prints and cartoons of the period, most of them poking fun at the Regent's relationship with his mistress, Lady Hertford. In an 1816 cartoon, a motley crowd of Londoners gathered around the cannon offer such observations as 'What an Erection to be sure!', 'I say, Nan, eight feet, what do you think of that!', and 'Dear heart, the very sight of it takes my breath away!'.

The chubby, dimpled cherubs swarming around the lamp-posts in Trafalgar Square seem to be enjoying the joke. They are a constant feature in London's streets. Two of the most interesting examples can be found in Temple Place on the Embankment, where you can admire a cheery little fellow pretty much *déshabillé* save for a telephone in which he is having an animated conversation, perhaps with another Heavenly being. He is listening through a receiver of the kind in use in the 1890s, when the lamp-post he decorates was erected. A companion figure is talking into the phone. The lamps flank the doorway of an imposing town house.

SUTTON HOUSE, HACKNEY

A stone's throw from the bustle of Hackney's Mare Street is the oldest domestic building in the East End of London, Sutton House, a remarkable Tudor survival.

It was built in the 1530s for one of Henry VIII's courtiers, Ralph Sadleir. A desirable red-brick mansion, the house was set in 30 acres of gardens and meadows sloping down to the banks of Hackney Brook, one of London's lost rivers. In those days it was just one of many grand houses built in Hackney, which in the 16th century was a fashionable retreat where courtiers and successful City merchants could enjoy the 'healthful air'. Now its neighbours are a car-repair yard, a primary school and a railway line. The traffic thundering past the front door does little for the once 'healthful air'.

The name Sutton House is a misnomer. Until recently it was widely believed that it had been the home, in the early 17th century, of the fabulously wealthy Thomas Sutton, founder of the Charterhouse Hospital and School. However, plans and deeds in the Charterhouse archives show that Sutton lived next door, in an old tan-house demolished in 1805 to make way for the fine Georgian terrace known as Sutton Place, which boasts some of the largest and most beautiful door-knockers in London.

The history of Ralph Sadleir's 'bryck palace' is closely bound up with that of Hackney itself. At different times it has been the home of James I's Master of the Rolls, a Venetian with the gloriously improbable name of Sir Julius Caesar; the residence of a flamboyant 17th-century silk merchant, Captain Milward; a boarding school; a trade union headquarters; and a squatter's paradise, where rock music regularly rattled the ancient timbers.

In 1938 Sutton House was acquired by the National Trust and rented out as offices. In a room decorated with rare Tudor 'linen' panelling Clive Jenkins, general Secretary of ASTMS, had his headquarters. By the early 1980s, however, the house stood empty and vandalised. Plans to sell it to property developers were opposed by local residents, and the National Trust eventually launched a project to restore the building for community use.

The process was one of constant discovery. Every surface concealed earlier features. The archaeological investigation uncovered a Tudor well, privy and fireplace, Jacobean wall-paintings and an 18th-century cesspit. Now visitors can open doors and panels to discover these features for themselves. Above the fireplace in the Georgian Room a panel swings open to reveal a Tudor graffito of a little man wielding a rattle to ward off the Devil. Rub him gently for good luck. Even the 400-year-old cobwebs in the Tudor privy have been left undisturbed, as has a baleful red eye painted in one of the upper rooms in the 1970s by an anonymous squatter.

In the richly panelled Great Chamber a portrait of Ralph Sadleir's grandson, extravagantly ruffed and with a hawk on his arm, occupies pride of place. Around him is an array of architectural features representing the changes in fashion and design over Sutton House's long history. The most recent additions include an elegant modern conference- and concert-hall, café-bar and art gallery, all of which enable Sutton House to be used for a wide range of contemporary purposes without disturbing its historic atmosphere.

Sutton House is at 2–4 Homerton High Street, E9. Railway: Hackney Central. For more information ring 0181 986 2264.

TEMPLE BAR

Take the train from Liverpool Street to Turkey Cross and a stiff walk to Theobalds Park, Cheshunt (in Hertfordshire, on the northern edge of London), will bring you to the last resting place of a famous landmark designed by Sir Christopher Wren.

Stranded in woodland is a dilapid ted archway ringed by a fence. This is Temple Bar, designed by Wren in 1672 to separate Fleet Street from the Strand and for over 200 years the official western entrance to the City of London. Carriage traffic passed through its large central arch and there are foot posterns at either side. It was decorated with figures of Charles I and Charles II, on the west side, and James I and Anne of Denmark on the east. Less pleasing were the remains of traitors displayed to the populace from Temple Bar. In 1684 various bits of Sir Thomas Armstrong's anatomy (boiled in salt so that the birds would not peck at them) were hung from the arch. Later Temple Bar played host to the heads of the Rye House plotters, impaled on spikes. Street vendors did brisk business, hiring out telescopes at a halfpenny a peek. The last head exhibited on Temple Bar was that of the Jacobite Francis Townley in 1746.

Beside the gate was a pillory in which Titus Oates in 1685 and Daniel Defoe in 1703 spent several uncomfortable days. Defoe had been imprisoned and pilloried for his satire *The Shortest Way with the Dissenters*. Unfortunately, he laid on the irony a little too thickly, and his absurd parody of extremist ideas landed him in the pillory. Ever the resourceful hack, Defoe turned this disagreeable experience to advantage with another successful work, *The Hymn to the Pillory*.

In 1806 Temple Bar was repaired and covered in black velvet for the funeral of Nelson. Between 1877 and 1878 growing traffic congestion caused its removal and for ten years it lay in pieces in a yard in the Farringdon Road until Sir Henry Bruce Meux re-erected it on his estate at Theobalds Park. Temple Bar is now in a very dilapidated condition, but the echoes of its great and grisly past still hang in the air around it.

Railway: Turkey Cross

TEMPLE OF MITHRAS

Now it's a collection of forlorn stones in the City at Temple Court, Queen Victoria Street, but once it was the Roman Temple of Mithras, a god with an ancient cult whose secrets are lost in the mists of time.

The existence of a temple to the Persian god Mithras had been suspected since 1889 when the relief of the god ritually slaughtering a bull was discovered in the Walbrook. The Walbrook is one of London's lost streams, rising in Finsbury and

flowing through the City into the Thames. The
Romans founded their settlement around the stream
and used it as their water supply. By 1383, however,
it was reported as being 'stopped up by divers filth
and dung'. By the 16th century it had disappeared
underground.

In Roman times, when it was still mercifully free
of dung, a temple dedicated to Mithras had been
built on its banks. Confirmation of its existence
came in 1954 when Professor W. F. Grimes secured
permission from the insurance company Legal &
General to explore the site on which a huge new
office block, Bucklersbury House, was about to rise.

Digging a trench across the ancient stream-bed
of the Walbrook, Grimes stumbled on a small
temple built in about AD 240 and dedicated to
Mithras, the god of heavenly light. Little is known
about the beliefs of his devotees. They seem to have
observed a strict moral code, with military men,
merchants and officials figuring in their ranks.
Water, fire and sacrifice played an important part in
their ritual.

The temple was small, 60-foot long and 26-foot
wide, and its layout resembled a Christian church,
with aisles and a row of columns on either side of a
narrow nave. It was probably attached to a private
house. Some time in the 4th century Mithras seems
to have fallen out of favour with Londoners, who
buried the temple's treasures. Their discovery by
Grimes caused a sensation sufficient to prompt
Legal & General to give him extra time to re-erect

the temple on the plinth which sits on the roof of their basement car park.

Grimes' finds are of great beauty. There is a head of Mithras, fleshy and full-lipped and exhibiting the signs of burning which might be connected with the use of fire in the worship of the god. Another find was a head of Serapis, the Egyptian god of the underworld, with a corn measure perched on his head. Perhaps the most mysterious find was a beautiful silver box decorated in relief with an elephant, snake, lion, hippopotamus, deer and wild boar as well as a number of more enigmatic mythical animals, possibly griffons tearing away at the lids of coffins. The box also contains an insert, perforated at the bottom, which might have been used for straining or infusing. These and other objects can be seen on display in the Museum of London.

The Temple of Mithras is at Temple Court, 11 Queen Victoria Street, EC4
Tube and Railway: Blackfriars

THEATRE ROYAL, DRURY LANE

If you sit under the magnificent dome of the Theatre Royal in Drury Lane, your eye will be drawn to the legends over the entrances to the auditorium. One, next to a toga-clad statue of David Garrick, who made his debut in the Theatre Royal in 1742, reads 'King's Side'. The other, guarded by Edmund Kean as Hamlet, gloomily contemplating Yorick's skull, reads 'Prince's Side'.

The legends refer to a unique feature of Drury Lane, which is the only theatre to boast two royal boxes. Towards the end of his long reign, the much put-upon George III was involved in a violent altercation in the theatre's foyer with his eldest son, the Prince of Wales. The Prince was roaring drunk, and his father boxed him about the ears. To prevent a recurrence of this unpleasantness, the management decided to build a separate box for the Prince of Wales to keep the warring royals apart – a lesson for our own times, perhaps.

It was at the Theatre Royal that another of George III's sons, the Duke of Clarence, first saw Mrs Dorothy Jordan, the Irish actress who became his mistress and bore him several children. The Duke paid her an allowance of a thousand pounds a year. When the King demanded that this be halved, a shamefaced Clarence informed Mrs Jordan. The spirited woman sent for a Drury Lane playbill and pointed to the words at the bottom, which read, 'No Money Returned After the Rising of the Curtain'.

When the Theatre Royal was rebuilt in 1794, it was equipped with an iron safety curtain, the first of its kind. On the opening night the audience was given a demonstration of its efficacy as they settled into their seats. A stagehand paraded in front of them hammering away at the safety curtain like a railwayman tapping the wheels of a locomotive. A further treat was in store. Over the stage were suspended two giant water tanks, the 18th-century equivalent of sprinklers, which were invisible to the audience. As the safety curtain was raised, water cascaded into a third tank on the stage. When the waters subsided, another stagehand sculled across the artificial lake in a rowing boat.

Sadly, these precautions failed to prevent Drury Lane from being consumed by fire in 1809. The flames could be seen from the House of Commons, where the playwright Richard Brinsley Sheridan, a former manager of the theatre and then an MP, was attending a debate. Later Sheridan, who had invested everything he owned in the theatre and thus faced ruin, was observed sipping a glass of port and watching the blaze from a nearby tavern. When friends tried to pull him away, he protested, 'No, leave me, 'tis a pity if a man cannot enjoy a glass of wine by his own fireside'. Present patrons of the Theatre Royal need not worry. Today's safety curtain weighs over 20 tons.

Poor George III could have had few happy memories of the Theatre Royal. In 1800 he survived an assassination attempt there. Something else is calculated to give the unwary a jolt at Drury Lane – its ghost, the 'Man in Grey'. Unlike most ghosts, he does not announce his presence with a sudden chill and is welcomed by harassed producers as a good omen, legend having it that he is most often seen during long runs. His name refers to the grey riding coat which he wears, his elegant attire completed by a powdered wig and three-cornered hat. A creature of habit, he invariably materialises at Row D in the Upper Circle, moves along the back, passes the bar and then melts through a wall on the far side of the auditorium. An intensely private ghost, his features and outline immediately become indistinct if anyone tries to approach him. Musicals seem to bring him out most often, usually during matinées. During the Second World War he was spotted wafting along his usual way while an air raid raged outside.

A story goes that some 19th-century workmen dug a male skeleton out of the wall near the scene of the Man in Grey's perambulations. A dagger was lodged in his side and the tatters of richly brocaded cloth hanging from the bones suggested that he was a man of wealth. Perhaps he was the rich admirer of an actress done to death by a jealous former lover. Of one thing we can be certain; casts and technicians at the Theatre Royal will be delighted if he continues his wraith-like progress through-the auditorium.

Tube: Covent, Garden

THAMES WATER TOWER,
SHEPHERD'S BUSH

Heraclitus, the pre-Socratic philosopher, would have understood that blight of modern urban planning, the roundabout. It was Heraclitus who stated that because all matter is in a state of perpetual change, 'You can never step in the same river twice'. This axiom would have applied perfectly to the traffic churning around Hyde Park Corner, an excellent example of fast-flowing, never-ending flux.

Roundabouts were originally conceived in France in 1907 by the civil engineer Henard, but they are now as British as shell suits and pot noodles (and about as aesthetically pleasing), the perfect expression of the get-out-of-my-way, road-crazy culture of recent years. Now, to make our roundabouts more agreeable obstacles to negotiate, fashionable artists are being commissioned to design exotic sculptures to adorn them.

The first, unveiled in January 1995, is the Thames Water Tower, a 70-foot glass and steel barometer, set at an angle like the Leaning Tower of Pisa, which decorates the previously joyless roundabout at Shepherd's Bush. Designed by Tanya Doufa and Damien O'Sullivan, both graduates of the Royal College of Art, the tall glass tower contains blue water levels which rise and fall inside as the barometric pressure changes. Nozzles inside the tower spray the blue water on to the glass, down which it runs to be collected and recirculated. Apart from being a wonderful, winking addition to a previously dreary urban landscape, the tower performs a severely practical function, hiding a tall, unsightly concrete relief pipe linked to the Thames

Water Ring Main (itself a huge roundabout of water charging at full tilt) which runs below.

Piped water is as vital to London's survival as an effecient sewage system. The city's first post-Roman water pipes, installed in the Middle Ages, were bored elm trunks, eight inches in diameter, tapered at one end to fit into each other. Examples of these early pipes can be seen, still in excellent condition, at the Kew Bridge Steam Museum (see p. 88). From these medieval tree trunks were derived the later expressions, 'trunk call' and 'trunk road'.

Since the mid-1800s London has had water supplied from water treatment works in the west and north-east of the capital through large-diameter iron trunk mains, many of which were laid over 100 years ago. As London's population and demand for water grew, water had to be pumped for distances of up to 18 miles, requiring an increase in pumping pressure at the works to maintain the flow. By the 1970s, however, age, pumping pressure and heavy traffic on the roads above were causing a worrying amount of leakage from the pipes. Ten years later the system was fast approaching the end of its useful life.

Digging down to replace all those mains would have produced chaos in London's streets. The problem was exacerbated by the fact that the spaghetti of pipes, tunnels and cables already beneath our feet meant that there was little or no room for new or replacement services. And because Londoners were using more water every year, it had become impossible to take trunk mains out of service for essential maintenance.

The answer, proposed in 1984 and completed in November 1994, was to build an 80-mile gravity fed concrete-lined tunnel, eight feet in diameter, in a loop around London at an average depth of 130 ft, deeper than most Tube lines. Wide enough to take a London taxi and running round the capital like an underground M25, the tunnel uses the principal of the electrical ring main to provide water supply from either direction in the 'ring'. If one section has to be shut down, the supply to other parts of London will not be affected.

Water pours into the tunnel from the major treatment works at a maximum rate of 285 million gallons a day – enough to fill the Albert Hall eight times. Eleven pumping stations, housed within strategically placed tunnel shafts, lift the water by gravity and pump it into the existing mains supply network. The construction of the Thames Water Ring Main involved the excavation of 1.2 million tons of earth by three 200-foot-long tunnelling machines which were capable of boring their way through a mile of London clay a month. The tunnel holds the world record for speed of tunnelling – 548 yards in ten days.

The Shepherd's Bush roundabout is at the junction of Holland Park Avenue and Holland Road, W12.

Tube: Shepherd's Bush
For more information on the Thames Water Tower
and Ring Main, Tel: 0734 399271

TIPPOO SAHIB'S TIGER

The Victoria & Albert Museum is one of the
wonders of London. A museum of fine and applied
art of all countries, styles and periods, it has proved,
in the words of former director Sir Roy Strong, 'an
extremely capacious handbag'. In its halls visitors
can admire exhibits as disparate as plaster casts of
Trajan's Column, Schiaperelli cocktail dresses with
surrealist designs by Salvador Dali, and the 12-inch
platform-heel shoes, designed by Vivienne West-
wood, in which supermodel Naomi Campbell took a
tumble on a Paris catwalk in 1993.

The Indian section contains one of the museum's
most intriguing items – a life-sized automaton of
carved and painted wood representing a ferocious
tiger devouring a prostrate European clad in dress
of the 1790s. A cranked handle operates two mech-
anisms, the first to move the man's jointed arm,
thrown up in a vain attempt to protect himself from
the rampaging beast, and the second to simulate
roars and grunts. A flap in the tiger's flank reveals
an organ keyboard which can be played to create the
effect of the man's dying screams.

This sanguinary tableau was the favourite toy of

Tipu Sultan, the 'Tiger of Mysore' and a doughty
foe of the British, who knew him as Tippoo Sahib.
Tipu met his own end at the Battle of Seringapatam
in 1799, and the cabinet which contains his tiger
also houses personal items taken from his body by
British officers, among them a sumptuous brooch, a
richly decorated watch made in London and a
telescope. A portrait of Tipu – plump and mousta-
chioed – sits beneath his wooden pet. Alongside is a
print of one of his 'rocket men', soldiers who carried
rockets, mounted on bamboo poles and filled with
cartridges, which had a range of up to half a mile.
The rocket man's distinctive uniform is decorated
with diamond-shaped patterns to suggest tiger
stripes.

*The Victoria & Albert Museum is on the Cromwell
Road, SW7*
Tube: South Kensington

TRADESCANT MUSEUM, LAMBETH

On the southern side of Lambeth Bridge stand two
large columns surmounted by pineapples. They are
reminders of the time, in the 17th century, when
sailors would mark their safe return from a voyage
in the tropics by hanging a pineapple on their front
doors.

John Tradescant, Charles I's gardener, tried unsuccessfully to cultivate pineapples at his house in Lambeth. He had more encouraging results with the many flowers, shrubs and trees he brought back from his travels to Europe and America. Tradescant was a great plant hunter. He was the first botanist to visit Russia, keeping a racy diary of his time there and returning with a rose which is still cultivated today.

Tradescant and his son John, who succeeded him as a royal gardener, were also avid collectors of 'all things strange and rare', displaying their collection of curiosities in their Lambeth house. Among the exhibits was a stuffed dodo, originally the last of its kind to be exhibited alive in England. The Tradescants' collection became a place of great educational interest and was visited by the Court and notabilities of the day. Ultimately, it formed the basis of the Ashmolean Museum in Oxford, where much of it can be seen today in the Founder's Room.

Both the Tradescants are buried in an elaborate tomb in the churchyard at St Mary's at Lambeth, next to Lambeth Palace. The sides of the tomb are alive with mythical and exotic beasts, including an impressive crocodile thrashing his tail. Next to the Tradescants is the tomb of William Bligh, another former resident of Lambeth (whose house is opposite the Imperial War Museum). Forever associated with the mutiny on the Bounty, he was also one of the great navigators and the man responsible for transplanting the bread-fruit to the West Indies.

In the mid-1970s, St Mary's lay in a sad state of
dereliction, grime-caked and open to the sky.
Thanks to the heroic efforts of husband and wife
John and Rosemary Nicholson, an appeal was
launched to save the church, which has been transformed into a unique museum of garden history, a
fitting memorial to the lives and work of the
Tradescants.

Inside the restored church, mellow stone walls
and rich stained glass look down on a range of
exhibits calculated to set the pulse of a keen gardener racing. There is a room devoted to the great
gardener Gertrude Jekyll, hawk-faced and formi-
dable in hairy tweeds. Another delight is a remarkable array of garden tools ranging from elegant 18th-
century copper watering-cans to 19th-century stick

tools, which resemble sword sticks but contain less life-threatening gardening implements. A collection of gardening books includes such delightful titles as the wartime *Cloches versus Hitler*. Serried ranks of antique lawn-mowers wait for summer days and lush lawns to cut.

Part of the churchyard has been turned into a replica of a 17th-century garden containing only plants grown by the Tradescants or other plants of the period. A peaceful fountain splashes away in a corner. Like John Tradescant's rose, the project continues to grow.

The Museum of Garden History is on Lambeth Palace Road, SE1
Tube: Lambeth North, Waterloo, Westminster.
Railway: Waterloo.
The museum is open from Monday to Friday, 11 a.m. to 3 p.m. and on Sunday from 10.30 a.m. to 5 p.m. The museum closes from the second Sunday in December to the first Sunday in March. For further information ring 0171 261 1891 (Monday to Friday 11 a.m. to 3 p.m.) or Answer Phone 0171 373 4030

TWININGS TEA SHOP,
THE STRAND

At the eastern end of the Strand are the premises occupied by the oldest ratepayers in the City of Westminster, Twinings the tea merchants.

The Twinings have been in the tea business since 1706. It was Richard Twining who turned the British into a nation of tea drinkers when in 1784 he persuaded the Prime Minister of the day, William Pitt, to slash the then punitive tax on tea. The Twinings shop at No. 216, with its golden lion and two reclining Chinamen over the door, was established in 1787. Inside it's long, cool and, at seven-foot wide, very narrow. Original portraits of the family line the walls. One of them depicts Mary Twining, the widow of Daniel Twining, who ran the business single-handed for 17 years after her husband died in 1762, a remarkable achievement for a woman in 18th-century London.

The story goes that the ritual of taking afternoon tea was started by the seventh Duchess of Bedford (1788–1861). The Duchess was irked by the desert between breakfast and dinner, the two main meals of the day, and seemingly unsatisfied by a light luncheon. She sustained herself with tea and sliced bread and butter taken in her boudoir at 4 p.m. Soon friends joined her in 'containing the pangs of hunger', and afternoon tea moved out of the boudoir and into the drawing-room.

This pleasant break quickly got a little out of

hand as the hostesses of the day strove to impress. Simple bread and butter was soon replaced by sandwiches with exotic fillings, scones, crumpets and cakes. The upper classes became 'China mad', using tea as an excuse for showing off their extravagant purchases of Chinese export porcelain and Dresden tea-sets.

Twinings has survived all the subsequent ups and downs of the tea trade, from the introduction of the tea-bag in the early 1900s to tea rationing during the Second World War, the introduction of which convinced the British that things were now getting really serious. Twinings are nothing if not adaptable. Their literature even contains a recipe for a tea cocktail, Highland Fling. Mix together two measures of double strength Twinings Assam tea, two measures of whisky and one measure of fresh lemon juice. Add sugar to taste and cool, then pour on to ice and top with dry ginger ale. Perfect after a sweltering summer's day.

At the back of Twinings' shop is a small museum devoted to the pleasures of tea. Its showpiece is a unique teapot, the biggest in the world, which serves 13 gallons of tea. Decorated with scenes depicting all the aspects of tea-making, it was made for the Great Exhibition of 1851 and, according to Twinings, dispensed a cup to an appreciative Queen Victoria and Prince Albert. Other exhibits include examples of exquisite 18th-century tea-caddies, an essential accessory when tea was still an expensive commodity drunk only by the wealthy. As a safety

precaution the caddies were provided with locks fashioned by skilled craftsmen, and the key was kept by the lady of the house.

Twinings' most expensive current line is Finest Oolong, which sells at just over £10 per pound. It's a delicious semi-fermented tea from Taiwan which tastes strongly of peaches.

Twinings' shop is at No. 216 the Strand, WC2
Tube: Aldwych

TYBURN

On the traffic island at the junction of the Edgware Road and the Bayswater Road, a stone marks the spot of one of the grimmest locations in London, the Tyburn gallows, the principal place of public executions in the capital from 1388 to 1783.

It was not until the summer of 1571 that permanent gallows were erected at Tyburn, for the hanging of John Story, 'a Romish Canonical Doctor'. Condemned prisoners were carried to Tyburn in a cart, and their progress was accompanied by a number of rituals. They were given a nosegay of flowers outside St Sepulchres, Holborn, while the bellman rang his bell and recited a verse calling for repentance and requesting the people's prayers for the 'poor sinner' going to meet his Maker. At the church of St Giles in the Fields the 'poor sinner' was given a last mug of ale.

As the magistrate and novelist Henry Fielding wrote in his *Inquiry into the Causes of the Late Increases in Robbers*, published in 1751, 'The day appointed by law for the thief's shame is the day of glory in his own opinion. His procession to Tyburn and his last moments there are all triumphant . . .' A century earlier a foreign observer wrote that those about to hang took great care over their physical appearance. Men shaved and were 'handsomely dressed either in mourning or the dress of a bridegroom . . . Sometimes the girls dress in white with great silk scarves and carry baskets full of oranges and flowers, scattering these favours all the way they go'.

The hanging was a rough-and-ready business. The cart stopped under the gallows and the noose was tied around the neck, whereupon the cart-horse was whipped on by the executioner, leaving the victims' legs kicking the air. The hangman did not bother to put them out of their agony; this unpleasant task was left to friends and relations, pulling at their legs or beating upon their chests. However, the hangman was entitled to the clothes of those he hanged. In 1447 this led to a macabre incident when five men had been hung, cut down while still alive and marked out for quartering. At this point a pardon arrived. The wretches recovered their senses but not their clothes, which the executioner refused to return. They walked home naked.

The day of a hanging was a public holiday, the aim being to provide the public with a spectacle designed to deter them from crime. But the atmosphere was more one of carnival than the solemn contemplation of retributive justice. When the legendary criminal Jack Sheppard was executed at Tyburn in 1714, an estimated 200,000 people turned out to watch. A Scottish clergyman observed that as a result of these spectacles, 'a great number were made worse rather than better . . . Of the ragamuffin class a large proportion were gratified by the sight; and within my hearing many expressed their admiration of the fortitude, as they termed the hardness and stupidity, of one of the sufferers . . .'

Hogarth caught the flavour of an 18th-century hanging at Tyburn in an engraving of 1747. In the foreground a seething mass of spectators strain for a view of the huge gallows, big enough to accommodate 21 bodies. Pickpockets and prostitutes jostle hawkers and sellers of gin and gingerbread; infants are trampled underfoot in the crush; and the quality watch from the comfort of a grandstand. Things tended to get even more chaotic after the hanging, when the crowd pressed forward to touch the corpses in the belief that they possessed medicinal properties. A shocked Frenchman wrote of a beautiful young woman, pale and trembling, who bared her breasts before the mob to enable a dead man's hand to caress them. After the hubbub had subsided and the bodies had been carted off for burial or dissection, the hangmen went to a tavern in Fleet Street where, between drinks, they sold off the rope at sixpence an inch.

Tube: Marble Arch

WHITECHAPEL BELL FOUNDRY

Behind the elegant classical façade of No. 32 Whitechapel Road lies the oldest manufacturing business in London, the Whitechapel Bell Foundry.

Four hundred years ago the sign of the three bells – the stamp of Robert Mot, master founder –

identified those bells cast in Whitechapel. Today's foundry stamp is based on Mot's trademark, but bell-founding in Whitechapel goes farther back, to the time of Robert Chamberlain, who was active in Aldgate around 1420.

Its long history has not prevented the foundry moving with the time. Recently it has introduced sophisticated electronic bell-tuning and developed computerised chiming devices and carillon control units.

Time, however, is a relative concept in the world of bell-founding. Some of Robert Chamberlain's bells survive, and there are still two bells in Westminster Abbey cast by Robert Mot in the 1580s. Sitting in his quiet panelled office, foundry director Alan Hughes, a fourth-generation bell-founder, talks about events two or three hundred years ago as if they happened last week. In the yard outside, old bells lay up-ended waiting decisions on their future which may take 20 or more years to make.

The foundry's history rings with the sound of famous bells. London's 'Bow Bells' were cast here between 1738 and 1752. Whitechapel's largest bell was 'Big Ben', weighing in at just over 13 tons. The 19th-century ledgers show that Whitechapel was often turning out three complete peals a month. The pace of modern bell-founding has slowed to three complete peals a year, but the foundry has a secure future. Its bells can be found as far afield as Miami and Wogga Wogga (over half of Australia's tower bells were cast in Whitechapel), a tribute to more than five-and-a-half centuries of craftsmanship.

The Foundry is not open to the public but the façade and charming shop at the front in No. 32 Whitechapel Road can be admired.
Tube: Whitechapel

Entries by Area

E1
Old Operating Theatre and Museum
Whitechapel Bell Foundry

E3
Hanging the Bun

E9
Sutton House

E15
Abbey Mills Pumping Station

EC1
Betjeman's Mural
Bunhill Fields
House of Detention
Postman's Park

EC3
Cornhill Devils

EC4
Apothecaries' Hall

All Pan Books are available at your local bookshop or newsagent, or can be ordered direct from the publisher. Indicate the number of copies required and fill in the form below.

Send to: Macmillan General Books C.S.
                Book Service By Post
                PO Box 29, Douglas I-O-M
                IM99 1BQ

or phone: 01624 675137, quoting title, author and credit card number.

or fax: 01624 670923, quoting title, author, and credit card number.

or Internet: http://www.bookpost.co.uk

Please enclose a remittance* to the value of the cover price plus 75 pence per book for post and packing. Overseas customers please allow £1.00 per copy for post and packing.

*Payment may be made in sterling by UK personal cheque, Eurocheque, postal order, sterling draft or international money order, made payable to Book Service By Post.

Alternatively by Access/Visa/MasterCard

Card No.

Expiry Date

Signature   _____

Applicable only in the UK and BFPO addresses.

While every effort is made to keep prices low, it is sometimes necessary to increase prices at short notice. Pan Books reserve the right to show on covers and charge new retail prices which may differ from those advertised in the text or elsewhere.

NAME AND ADDRESS IN BLOCK CAPITAL LETTERS PLEASE

Name _____

Address _____

_____

_____

_____

8/95

Please allow 28 days for delivery.
Please tick box if you do not wish to receive any additional information. ☐